CONVERSATIONS WITH Milton H. Erickson, M.D.

VOLUME 2

Changing Couples

CONVERSATIONS WITH Milton H. Erickson, M.D.

VOLUME 2

Changing Couples

Edited by

Jay Haley

TRIANGLE PRESS

First Edition

Printed in the United States of America

Library of Congress Catalog Card Number 84-052027

ISBN 0-931513-02-2

Published by Triangle Press
Distributed by W. W. Norton & Co., Inc., 500 Fifth Avenue, New York, N. Y. 10110
W. W. Norton & Co., Ltd., 37 Great Russell Street, London, WC1B3NU

CONTENTS

INTRODUCTION

These conversations with Milton H. Erickson, M.D., took place in the 1950s and 1960s when he was developing a new approach to therapy. Many aspects of therapy were discussed with him over those years. I have selected for this volume conversation about his therapy with marital couples. Other volumes deal with individuals and with children and their families. Naturally, when talking about individuals or families, issues of marriage come up, but in this volume the focus is particularly on the topic of marriage.

The conversations with Dr. Erickson were mostly conducted by John Weakland and myself with, at times, Gregory Bateson joining us. The study of this approach to therapy was part of Bateson's research project on communication. John Weakland and I visited Erickson every year for many years to talk with him about the nature of hypnosis and about how to do therapy. When he passed through the San Francisco area, the Bateson project always met with him to inquire into his ideas and his work. Bateson was often present at those interviews. We had the view at that time that an understanding of human communication could come out of the study of the process of changing that communication.

These conversations were not conducted with publication in mind but for research purposes. Therefore, they are not a selection designed to present Erickson's ideas to the world. The fact that these recordings exist made it possible to transcribe them and present his work in his own words. Our interest in talking with him was to explore the nature of communication and to answer specific research questions. John Weakland and I were also in practice as therapists and so our interests were practical as well as scientific.

Within the topic of the therapy of marital couples, I have selected conversations with Erickson from different times and put them together in as coherent a sequence as possible. The interviews with him covered many topics and were done at different times with many interruptions for patients, telephone calls, and periods of time between meetings. The reader might wish that a topic, which was abruptly dropped, had been pursued, but because of circumstances it was not.

At the time these conversations began Erickson and his therapy was so unique that it was difficult for us to understand. The standard psychodynamic therapy of the time assumed the therapist was a non-directive, passive listener. In that framework Erickson's therapy seemed different and strange and we struggled to understand what would seem more obvious, at least to us, a decade or two later. Although he was in isolation at the time of these conversations, in the sense of doing a therapy different from his colleagues, since that time the field has gone in his direction and seeing couples and families, as well as doing a directive strategic therapy, is assumed to be the correct way to change people.

Except for editorial corrections and the arrangement of the conversations from different times, the interviews are verbatim. What is here is what was said. The research-minded will find a copy of the original recordings of these conversations on file with the Erickson Foundation in Phoenix.

Readers familiar with my book, *Uncommon Therapy* (Norton, 1973), will find familiar cases since some of these conversations were the raw data on which I based that book.

CHAPTER 1

Love and Marriage

1959. Present were Milton H. Erickson, Jay Haley, and John Weakland.

Haley: If you were to describe what a good marriage is, how would you describe it?

Erickson: When I describe a good marriage to my patients, I point out to them that there are essentially four kinds of love. The infantile type of love, "I love me." The next stage, "I love the me in you. I love you because you are my brother, my mother, my father, my sister, my dog. The *me* in *you*." Then the adolescent type of love, "I love you because your dancing pleases me, and because your beauty pleases me, and because your brains please me." And the adult stage of love wherein, "I want to love you and cherish you because I want to see you happy because I can find my happiness in your happiness. The happier you are, the happier I'll be. I'll find my happiness in yours. I'll find delight in your pleasure and intellectual pursuits. I'll find a delight in your enjoyment of dancing." So, the mature love is the capacity to find enjoyment in the enjoyment of the other person's enjoyment. It works both ways.

H: Just what do you think a good marriage is composed of, or what a good marriage is? That is, you see things wrong with a marriage in contrast or against a background of what's good.

E: Yes. So in a good marriage you'll see some of the, "I love me." You should expect that. You'll see some of the, "I love the me in you." You'll see some of the adolescent variety of your good qualities that please *me*. But there should be a very considerable percentage of the enjoyment of the other person's state of happiness. It isn't enough just to enjoy your wife's cooking. You ought to enjoy the pleasure she has *in* cooking. You ought not just enjoy the fact she keeps the kids quiet while you're working. You want to enjoy, really, the pleasure and satisfaction she gets out of dealing with the kids, even though you can't understand why that particular dealing with the kids gives her so much satisfaction. It's beyond your capacity to understand, but you're so glad she enjoys it. You know that as long as she's happy, enjoying the inexplicable things, you're going to be happy too. I point out to couples that happiness in marriage so often depends on giving the other person the privilege of enjoying those special, peculiar pleasures that they have. Enjoying the fact that the other person is happy. You see, it's the being mature, the adult stage, that I emphasize. I look for that sort of thing. A woman who says, "I just can't understand my university professor of anthropology husband enjoying those completely stupid western movies. But for some strange and inexplicable, infantile reason he likes them. I know all the particular actors that please him most, and I always see to it that I tell him when one of his favorite actors is going to appear in a western." She just can't understand it. But she takes a great deal of pleasure in letting him have that pleasure, which to her is infantile and stupid. But it's so nice for her husband to be happy. It's such a harmless thing. It's a time-limited thing. He never goes to excess, but he so thoroughly enjoys that.

H: Well, certainly a common marriage problem that I see is when one starts to enjoy something, the other can't seem to tolerate it.

E: Yes. So many marital problems are built around the idea, "We must share equally in all things." I point out so quickly, so thoroughly, to them that you can't share equally in all things, because biologically we're totally different creatures. I emphasize the biological differences, which can't be disputed – the individual difference, the fact that he was attracted to her because she was biologically different and had different qualities. Then I point out that for the benefit of the children – and parents do wish their children well – that they want their children to have the advantage of every possible opportunity. If father and mother both go out of the home and bring back precisely the same thing, the children may get an adequate supply of the same thing. But if mother goes out and brings home something, and father goes out and brings home something different, the children have a choice of two things. So mother goes out and takes in the Russian ballet, and she comes back and tells the little children about the beauties of the ballet. Father goes out and looks at the desert landscape and really enjoys that, and the children listen to that. So the children have the opportunity of learning to like both the ballet and the landscape.

H: Well, what you look for in this enjoying the other's enjoyment is some degree of autonomy of each one while in a relationship.

E: Now and then you run across pathological sharing. A couple came to me, both had been unhappily married before, got divorces, and when they met they decided they would share everything. Well he liked westerns, and she liked musical comedies. So they went to the show twice a week – one western, one musical comedy. She gritted her teeth throughout the western, and he gritted his teeth throughout the musical comedy. They both comforted themselves that they were sharing. I pointed out, "You're sharing a common drama. As I understand it, your husband really enjoys that western, and you sat there hating it and gritting your teeth. What sharing were you doing? You weren't even sitting in the same seat that he was, you weren't sharing anything except proximity." I pointed out to them how nice it would be, and I hauled in the paper showing them, here's a western, here's a musical comedy. This theater on that side of the street, and this theater on this side of the street. Why don't you go, instead of gritting your teeth, and really enjoy what you see on the screen. You can go at such and such a time, the movie's over at such and such a time. You come out of the movie, you join each other, and you go for sandwiches. You have shared a delightful evening. They couldn't see it that way. When she went to the bathroom, he went to the bathroom. They shared. (Laughter) They always ate the same thing. They went to bed at the same hour. They shared everything. Now they're divorced. They couldn't stand their sharing. Now that's an exaggerated type of pathological sharing, but autonomy is so tremendously important because the happy marriage is one in which you have this individual accomplishing certain things, that individual accomplishing certain things. Each for the self there. Then you have the individuals separately accomplishing certain things for the other. Then you have the two individuals accomplishing things together.

H: I wonder what you'd say about what goes wrong besides pathological sharing; what goes wrong with a marriage?

E: Some people grow up in the conviction of the goodness of their ideas. How many homes teach the goodness of their ideas? There is only one religious faith, you know, absolutely only one. And anyone of intelligence would naturally send his sons and his children to Podunk College. No other college in the U.S. is fit to be attended, just Podunk College. In how many homes do you have that type of thinking? So they marry, and the woman comes from Pumpkin Center College and the man comes from Podunk College. They never learn to respect the goodness of separate ideas.

H: If a wife has an idea, Pumpkin City College, and the husband has the idea, Podunk College, where they get into difficulty is when they try to influence each other.

E: Yes.

H: That's when they get in a struggle and marital battles.

E: And how many struggles are there? What is the name of that island in Delaware where big enders, little enders, and that controversy on which end of the egg should you break first. The complete oversight that you break an egg for the purpose of eating it. That momentous question that brought about internecine war – the two political points of view. The big enders and the little enders about how to crack a boiled egg. I try sometimes when I can't get anywhere in getting the patients to understand, letting them set up opposite camps. Whether, for example, on December 5th should they go out picnicking on the Birdie River, or go to the Arboretum; and the couple just arrayed against each other on that debate. They really battled that question. Where did they go on that day that I had picked out for them? I knew where they were going to go. They had had over a month's battling. They attended the Phoenix rodeo.

H: You mean you picked the day of the rodeo? (Laughter)

E: I picked the day of the rodeo, knowing that they would attend. Then we went over that very, very bitter battle. Shall it be the Birdie River or the Arboretum? Why make an issue of it?

Weakland: This is a demonstration of how pointless that battle is, is it not?

E: It's a proof demonstration, utterly surprising. They battled up to the time they suddenly realized that it was rodeo day. (Laughter) Then I raised the question of how many other things do you take divergent points of view on and miss the rodeos because sometimes you get too absorbed to see the rodeo that's coming along. Because it isn't as plain and easily recognizable as the Phoenix rodeo. There's so many little things of that sort that you can do. If you can't get them to recognize the futility and absurdity of diverse points of view, to settle the future, then you let them encounter a reality situation.

H: You seem to have a set of premises about what's a good marriage and what's a bad marriage. We wondered if you could lay those out reasonably clearly.

E: The major premise is this: that there *is* such a thing as a good marriage. And what is a good marriage for you would be a bad marriage for me. What would be a good marriage for me would be a bad marriage for you. In other words, the premise is that there is a good marriage possible for each and every one of us. "What kind of a good marriage do you want, that is compatible with you? You know very well that if you hadn't married your husband, with your own natural proclivities, you would have married someone else. Your marriage to A would lead to one kind of a good marriage. Your marriage to B would lead to another kind of good marriage. Or, if your marriage to A would lead to a bad marriage, it would be a different kind of a bad marriage than the marriage to B. Because A is one person; B is a totally different one." So you offer these premises. "Now can a bad marriage be turned into a good marriage? By alteration of your desires and wishes. You can have your mouth all set for filet mignon, and then you'll find that they have oysters on the menu. Now in your marriage, this marriage of yours, you wanted certain things. Apparently they are not there. What are the things that *are* there? No one person ever exploits *all* the possibilities of a marriage. The richness of your own personality belongs to *you*. It's going to take your spouse quite a long time, if ever he succeeds, in doing something to discover all the richness of your personality. The same holds true for him. It'll take you a long time. What are the things you want?"

H: Well, granted that it is from one point of view an individual matter, still I think you must have some ideas about how any two people relate to each other in a way that's going to make a problem, and how any two people don't but relate in some other ways.

E: You seem to think that there should necessarily be a problem. In ordinary everyday life with your friends, you're very careful not to mention, with certain friends, certain political questions, certain religious questions. When I visit one of my friends in New Orleans, somehow or other we have extensive conversations and never mention the racial problem. It just never happens to come up.

H: I'm not saying there has to be problems . . .

E: I think that in marriage each of the parties ought to be aware of the fact that there are certain blindnesses that are incomprehensible, and that you just do not make an issue or a problem of it.

H: Let me put it another way. Suppose in a week, or in a period of time, you have eight couples come in, or at least eight problem marriages come in, and you wanted to say how these were similar, granted the great variation of individuals. What was similar about the problems?

E: I usually feel that there is too much effort on the part of one spouse to convert the other spouse.

W: Yes, well that fits with what Milton was saying a minute ago about the positive. What I got from it was—make the most of what is there instead of looking for something else.

H: Yes.

E: You can have a completely delightful friendship with somebody who stupidly votes the wrong ticket. (Laughs) Who idiotically goes to the wrong church. Who criminally, wrongly, takes a false attitude on racial matters. But you can have an absolutely delightful friendship. In marriage you ought to wonder *why* your spouse can be so silly, idiotic; but every artichoke has those petals that are discarded. The only way you can enjoy the artichoke is by heaping up the discard, and ignoring it. Being grateful for that nice delightful, delicious, soft, base of the petal.

H: So the reform, or the effort to convert, is one of the things you see that they have in common.

E: They have in common. And the insistence on the *right* to convert. That's in error. They have the right to think that they can convert. But then they ought to recognize so does the other person have that same right. That establishes a stalemate. Well, why center your life around a stalemate? And there are so many other things. You see, I think therapy is primarily a matter of getting people to function adequately within a reality framework. The reality framework is that of eating and living and responding today, in today's realities, in preparation for tomorrow. I can think of one of my friends who is in his 28th year of analysis. (Laughter) He is earnestly seeking to understand his conflict. He desparately wants to fall in love, to marry, to have a home and children. He's desperately seeking to find out what sort of conflict prevents him from doing that. He's past 60 now. The calendar says that he can't fall in love. The calendar says he won't have children. But he's paying his analyst for five hours a week, exploring the question. All he has to do is look at the calendar. I told him back in 1934, "Listen, by 1940 you will have all the answers. If you're not married by 1940, you never, never will be married." Now I know he took what I said up with his analyst. In fact, he's taken it up with several analysts. You see, he's outlived his analyst. (Laughter) But the coming around of the year 1940, good heavens, if he didn't say, "I do," by that time, that ends it. You get these men in their late 40s who come in to you so pitifully. They tell you, "I went to college, I postponed marrying that nice high school girl until after I got through college. By that time she was married. In fact she was married by the time I was a sophomore in college. So I got engaged to a girl in college, but I postponed marriage until after I graduated. She married someone else. I got engaged another time. We postponed marriage until after I got suitably placed. She married someone else. All my life I've wanted a wife, a home, and children. I never did get suitably placed. I've never forgotten my desire. Now I'm 48. I've got a job working for my brother as a hired man on his cotton ranch. I met a nice woman, she's a widow, she hasn't had any children. She's had her menopause. Would it be all right for me to marry her?" My question was, "What else can you do? You're 48. You *could* marry a girl in her 20s or 30s and make her pregnant, but you never can join with her in 20- or 30-year-old anticipations for family; you're 48. If you've been afraid of marriage, and wife, and children all these years, you better pay respect to that fact. You say this woman you want to marry is 46. She's through her menopause, and she was never pregnant. She and her husband postponed pregnancy. I think you two have a great deal in common." I saw the brother about a year after the marriage. I asked how the married couple were getting along. He said, "There's been a transformation in my brother; he's actually become ambitious. He and his wife are working very nicely and they're building up a nice home. It's the center of the community so far as the children of the neighborhood are concerned." A safe way of having children. I don't know how many community projects she entered into which centered around children. So did he. Now why should I, in handling that couple, why should I go into all that horrible delaying about marriage, the avoidance on the part of both of them? You're going to live today, tomorrow, next week. Just thumping on the forces that entered into their 20s and 30s would serve no purpose. I think it's awfully important for them to live *today* and take care of the Girl Scout troop or the Boy Scout troop, and trick-or-treats on Halloween.

H: One of the things that I've come to conclude, somewhat reluctantly, is that helping a patient understand himself, become more aware of himself, has nothing to do with changing him.

E: Not one bit!

H: Well, I thought you would agree with that. (Laughs) It is bedrock to most psychiatry. They don't know how to talk to a patient unless it's to make him more self-aware.

E: Make them more self-aware, but they never do get the patient to become aware of the things he *can do*.

H: I notice how rarely you try to work on *why* a patient does anything, as if you consider it irrelevant *why* he does something.

E: Well, look over the lives of a lot of happy, successful, well-adjusted people and ask them why. (Laughter) It's so nonsensical. They're happy, they're well-adjusted, they like their work, they have got a joy of living. Why should we analyze their childhood, parental relationships. They've never bothered and they are never going to bother.

H: But apparently even at the couple level, if you see a couple in a struggle with each other, you don't attempt to work with them on why they have these attitudes toward each other at all?

E: Once in a while, you see a situation – I'm trying to think of one – where you better give them insight.

H: Well, can you differentiate those from others?

E: I'm trying to call to mind some specific case. Maybe I will later. But now and then with a patient or a couple, you better give them insight. Not on everything but on certain items.

H: Now, by "insight" do you mean why they're doing something they're doing?

E: Yes. A good deep analytical interpretation, understanding.

H: Well, if a patient does, as so many do, say, "I want to know why I'm afraid to go up a tall building." And they are constantly working on why they have the problems that they have, what do you do? You shift them away from the why, I gather?

E: I shift them away from the *why*. "Will you tell me *why* you would want to go up in a tall building? Have you got one single legitimate reason for going up there?" (Laughter) I think that's much more important than having to devote their lives to "being very careful to remember every day, every hour of the day, that they're afraid to go up in the tall building." You know, a patient came here to live in Phoenix to get therapy from me because of this fear of tall buildings. One thing in particular that troubled him were three-story houses.

H: There haven't been any of those for quite a while. (Laughter)

E: My statement was, "You have rented houses. You've been afraid to buy a house because of three-story houses. I want you to go out with pencil and notebook and record the address of every three-story house you see. (Laughter) That way you will be able to keep away from them." (Laughter)

H: Did he find any?

E: I told him, to help him out, "You'll find one up in Peoria here about 20 or 30 miles away." (Laughter) Then I named another one, and there's no way to get that one. "Those are places you can't possibly buy—you haven't got the money for it."

* * *

E: I can think of a 60-year-old doctor; 30 years ago he was all excited. He had a brand new office, and he was going to start up in practice. He was so excited that morning that he was a little bit late, and he wanted to be there on time so he had one fried egg, two slices of bacon, a slice of toast, and a cup of coffee. But he didn't have time to sit down and eat, so he just ate the egg, the two slices of bacon, the toast, and drank his coffee standing up at the table. He has been late to breakfast every morning for 30 years. He has had egg, two slices of bacon, toast and a cup of coffee, eaten standing up because he's late for the office. The question that floored him was, "Even now that you practice medicine very intensively, get to the office just about on time, always about five minutes late, you get home what time in the late evening?" About 10 o'clock, 11 o'clock, between 10 and 11." He has an enormous practice. "Why didn't you marry the girl you were in love with?" He said, "Well, if I had married the girl I was in love with, we would have encountered expenses in the matter of children, things of that sort, and I wanted to build my practice. So I married another girl I wasn't in love with, because I knew I wouldn't handicap myself financially with children. I always knew that I could divorce her and marry someone I was in love with." And I said, "All right, now you've got an enormous practice. You're in the office from 8 in the morning to 10 or 11 at night, does your nurse or your receptionist or your secretary bring in that sandwich?" He said, "The secretary is pretty busy, so I have the receptionist, because my secretary can double as a receptionist." He comes home, and he eats at 10:30. He eats a meal his wife has prepared for him, goes to bed. A perfectly enormous practice. He practices medicine seven days a week. I said, "Now, besides your insurance do you have any other property?" He said, "No, except the house in which I live." I said, "Your insurance on the house in which you live, the total value of that is what?" He said, "Approximately $70,000." I said, "On what wildcat schemes did you waste your earnings?" He said, "Well, there's a mail order oil well up in Canada, a mail order oil well in Texas. Then there is that uranium mine, mail order, in Canada." I said, "What was the smallest sum you ever sunk into each of those?" "Well, never less than $20,000." When he saved up $20,000, he invested it. But you know immediately when he tells you that simple little thing about that breakfast of his, what all the rest of his life is going to be like. When he married a girl he didn't love because to marry the girl he did love would mean children, that man's going to have a life of self-defeat. You know immediately what the rest of the story is, you have to speculate on the particular form it takes. You know he's not going to have accumulated any savings. Doctors always fall for mail order schemes; they *are* poor businessmen. Thirty years of that.

H: If you see a series of problem couples, one of the issues you see is that they are trying to reform each other, convert each other. Are there any other general problems in the way you look at what goes wrong with a marriage?

E: The couples that just simply can't tolerate each other. This doctor, for example, marrying a woman he didn't love—why on earth did *she* marry him? Her life has been one, literally, of poverty, disappointment, frustration; that late-evening meal that she serves him is always a disappointment to him. She never remembers to cook him the things he wants. He always eats the things he doesn't want that she has prepared for him. Here are two people that can't tolerate each other who are bound in a situation of punishment of each other, and self-punishment.

H: Well, there's the class of marriage where the couple can't tolerate each other yet they live together.

E: Yes.

H: A peculiar kind of a double—they tolerate each other but they don't.

W: On her side, why she would've made this choice—my guess would be something around she wasn't in love with him either, but she could see that he was an ambitious, intelligent, hardworking young man that would do things.

E: He's the outstanding doctor in three large communities. His office is always open.

W: So in a sense they both got what they picked all right.

E: But it's a . . . what is it that they've got?

W: That's it.

E: It's complete emptiness.

W: But they picked it really, both of them.

E: They fell into the habit of promoting it.

H: Let's take this another way. Suppose you went to a wedding and you talked to a young couple right after they were married. If you predicted that that marriage would go on the rocks, what would you base a prediction on?

E: Well, if I talked to the young couple and I thought the marriage was going to go on the rocks, I would predict it in such a way that they would both take exception to me . . .

H: I'm not talking now about how you would be treating them. But just in your own mind, how you would classify something being wrong with their marriage? I mean, suppose you had six young couples, just married today, come in here and you decided that two of them – this wasn't going to go, that they were going to go on the rocks. I wonder what sort of things you would be looking for to make that prediction?

E: The exploitation of the one by the other. I can think of a marriage where there was a very nice, ornate wedding, and then after the wedding the bride said, "You know, my very best friend comes from a very poverty-stricken situation. She has never had a chance to travel. Since we're traveling by plane, why not give her a present of a plane trip with us? She doesn't even have to sit in the same part of the plane with us. We're going to such and such a city, she can take a motel on the other side of town. She can have a very nice, pleasant trip. If we want to, we can invite her to have dinner with us occasionally, go swimming with us occasionally." Well, there's a marriage you know right away is going to fail. The bridegroom consented. He had some money.

W: Then you really know. If you not only get this deal proposed but the other one buys.

E: You know right then.

W: Yes. That just sort of puts the seal on it.

E: A month later I was explaining to both of them which lawyer they ought to go to. (Laughter) But it's perfectly apparent. You see other marriages where you look at it, and you say, "Well, that marriage is going to fail." Here's this bride, insists that the bridegroom have, as his best man, the man she used to date, whom she wanted to marry, and who walked out of the situation. She's going to see to it that she stands in front of the alter with the man she wanted to marry. Now that marriage is going to fail. In what way is it going to fail? It's going to fail in one of two ways: either break up, or the husband is going to find himself in a very peculiar role, quite possibly wearing a ruffled apron. (Laughs) You see that over and over again. Well, you know on the wedding day. I've got a family here, an old, well-established family. I've had grandpa and grandma, all the sons and daughters, all of the in-laws, and some of the grandchildren as my patients. Sonny No. 4 fell in love with this beautiful, wealthy, charming socialite. She was very popular. Of course, his father was wealthy, his mother was a socialite, a leader, from Phoenix. He got so drunk they had to postpone the wedding for an hour. Where was he on the birth of his first child? He was on a three-day drunk. Where was he on the birth of his second child? His wife went to the hospital, and he went to a motel with a mistress. The third child – his wife had raised such a row that he came to the hospital, held her hand, and so on. Then he disappeared for three days with another mistress. The fourth child – treated the same way.

Then his wife came to see me. She said, "I'm in love

with Joe. I want to stay married to him." Joe's statement was, "A man has to have some kind of freedom." When I went into that question, "Why were you drunk so that your wedding had to be delayed?" he said, "Well, I had to say goodbye to the boys." No sense of values. A few quick ones over the bar saying goodbye to the boys is much more important than his wedding hour. You're safe in predicting.

The promiscuous girl who falls in love with some nice guy. She dates the nice guy and she falls in love. She flatly refuses to go to bed with him. Her steady bed partner comes around at the usual nighttime hour and finds that she's put a bolt on the door. She talks to him through the door and says, "Go away, I don't ever want to see you again." She tells that to all her boyfriends. She's had a couple of dates with this nice guy. She's fallen for him. She's not going to go to bed with him. She just hopes and hopes and hopes. She dates him. Pretty soon he falls in love with her. You know the marriage is going to be successful. She has cut her patterns off. All that promiscuity has disappeared. She went and bought that bolt to put on her door. After a couple dates with a nice guy. That nice guy made a pass at her, and she warded it off very gently, nicely. She doesn't know, she mistrusts herself, she puts that bolt there, she talks through the closed door. She's taking no chances at all, and no effort is too small to be ignored. She goes through her wardrobe. Let's see, Bill liked this dress, Dick liked that one, Harry liked that one, Gerald liked that one—out in the garbage they can go. She hated to do it, she liked those dresses. She starts looking through her dresser and she puts out this souvenir and that souvenir and she literally cleans house. I think you can predict very safely.

I can think of Marie, practically a professional prostitute. That's the way she made her living. She liked the things that other men's money could buy. Then she met Donald. Marie came to me and told me all about her past life of promiscuity. Her willingness to accept an apartment as a mistress of some man, and slip out to other apartments of other boyfriends. Then she met Donald. She was tremendously attracted to him. She hunted up a job, she hunted up a cheap apartment, she moved into that. She left her mink stole, just got rid of everything. Then she told me, she said, "I don't even know if I'll ever see Donald again, but I want him." I really couldn't give her any advice. She was reacting naturally. Cutting herself off. She was very careful before she agreed to marry Donald to find out whether or not he wanted children. She raised with him the question she might be sterile, that he might be sterile. A couple that go into marriage hopefully go in not knowing what the future holds. She found out that Donald was perfectly willing to marry her and take the chance that she might be sterile, and take the chance that he might be sterile. They did have two children though. It's the attitude toward the marriage of how seriously they view what they are doing.

CHAPTER 2

Confidentiality, Domination, and the Absurd

1958. Present are Milton H. Erickson, Gregory Bateson, Jay Haley, and John Weakland.

H: When you deal with families, and you see one person separately, and another separately, and all of them together, how do you deal with the problem of private communication, of secrets between you and a family member?

E: I get sanctimonious about that. (Laughter) I explain very carefully to the patient that my interview is strictly confidential. I always keep interviews confidential. Certainly I am not going to discuss what we say to your father or your mother, your husband, your wife. *I* keep interviews confidential. I don't know what *you* will do. But whatever you do will be all right. You can handle it any way you want to. And you know, that's exactly what I'm going to tell your husband, that's exactly what I'm going to tell your wife, that's exactly what I'm going to tell your child. I've cleared myself with all of them. Now if they start discussing their interviews with each other, they've got to live up to *my* statement that would be *all right*. But they didn't hear me put that in.

B: Put which in?

E: That it will be all right. So they've got to justify their communications with each other, breaking the confidences, by making it all right. "I'm sure that whatever you do will be *all right*." They're under a tremendous burden there.

B: You mean they will, in fact, talk about the interview; they will keep those pieces quiet.

E: Quiet and peaceful in order to make it "all right." "I'm sure that whatever you do will be 'all right.' *I'll* keep it confidential." That gives them full permission. I told them I'll tell that to all the others. So they each know that the other's under the same obligation, and all that rivalry between them stimulates them to make things "all right."

H: That's a complicated one, Milton.

W: Yes.

H: You take the competition and concern about what each other is talking about and shift it to making things all right.

E: You know, I had a husband and wife say, "We've had our first decent talk with each other. We violated this confidential relation, but we've had our first decent talk." They made it "all right."

H: You accept it, I gather, if one family member says, "I want to see you." If they come to you out of the blue, so to speak, with a telephone call, and the wife says, "I want to see you alone, before you see my husband." You go along with that?

E: Oh, certainly.

H: Then how do you handle the husband feeling resentful because you and the wife must have gotten together against him before he even gets in there?

E: Oh I beat the husband to the punch. Because she usually hasn't told him that she wants to see me alone first. I tell her over the phone, "Yes, I'll see you alone first, but let me handle it and don't say anything at all about it." And so I go out and meet them where they're waiting. I say, "I can see one or the other of you first alone. That's the way I usually do things. I suppose I can do it this way. Ladies first." "If it's the husband who has asked, I say, "Well I suppose we can do it this way; we'll let your wife have the last word." (Laughter)

H: You're just full of these clichés for resolving these situations.

E: Those clichés are part of the language. So the husband, who has asked to see me first alone, doesn't want his wife to know. I've done his wife a favor of letting her have the last word. She's rather smug about it. The wife who has asked – I've just followed Emily Post; ladies first. "At least that's one psychiatrist that knows his Emily Post." Instead of it being a fixed-up, prearranged set-up.

H: Well, how do you handle it when you're seeing a family and the wife calls and talks to you on the phone about her husband, and she says she doesn't want her husband to know that she called?

E: That she has called? I tell her, "Well *I'm* not going to tell him, but if you get your husband here, you'll have to tell him something. If you want to come in and see me without your husband's knowledge, that's perfectly all right with me. It'll pose some problems, but I expect you can handle them."

H: That's on an initial contract. How about when you see them regularly and the wife calls you secretly, or the husband calls you secretly?

E: I've had them try to make me betray my hand by giving me information – to have me spill it to the other. I'm very careful about that. Because I don't know what they want when they do that. I keep my interviews confidential.

H: It's just that there's an emphasis among some people

who are interviewing families on "no private communication." Everything has to be open and aboveboard.

E: Well that's a dictatorial, autocratic, dogmatic statement. Of course, my description of it as such is not a dogmatic statement. (Laughter) But you have an open agreement with the family, "You know, sooner or later there's the possibility that some of our communications with each other should be confidential. Sooner or later it will be confidential. I know if the occasion arises with you, Mr. X, that you want that respected. In fact, I know if it arises with your wife, you want it respected."

W: In other words, Milton will handle this the same way as other things. He will put it under *his* hand from the outset.

E: Only because they want that thing respected.

W: I've got a question I'd like to ask. In treating a family, now say you have a couple when the man has come to you for therapy. But the wife says, "There's nothing wrong with me; I don't need therapy." She has that attitude. Now the therapist can bring her in by saying, "Well look, I think I need to talk to you about the trouble in your home," and so on. So then she always asks, "Are you treating *me*, doing therapy with me?"

E: Oh, I've beaten her to the punch.

W: Okay.

E: The woman says, "My husband is a bastard. I've lived with him 15 years and I know he is, and he needs therapy, and he needs a great deal of it. I don't need one particle of therapy. He needs it all." I can tell her, "I'll agree with you, your husband does need therapy. You know it and I know it. Now my job is to get him to understand that fact. But actually, of course, I'd like to do this as expeditiously as possible, so I'll have to have some interviews with you. Because I don't want to spend all the time that otherwise would be necessary getting, bit by bit, the information from him. So I'll need interviews with you." All of a sudden she comes out, "Are you treating me?" I say, "If you look over our interviews in which you gave me information about your husband, from time to time didn't you point out to me how hard it was for you to get along with your husband's misconduct and misbehavior? Do you think that you could maintain your equilibrium with a husband who is that ornery? Don't you think you need some advice on how to adjust to some of that behavior of your husband? Do you really think anybody could live with that bastard for 15 years and not show something wrong? Tell me honestly. Would anybody in her right mind live with him 15 years?" (Laughter) Do you see the type of question? She can tell me, "I think you're right. He's enough to drive anybody bats, and I've felt half bats many a time." It's a rather easy thing. You see when they attack me, I do not get defensive. Unless I can see a way of using it.

W: Well, what about the opposite?

E: What's that?

W: Becoming aggressive. Do you find a way to use that at times?

E: Oh yes. I have told a husband and a wife in interviews, "Now you've been battling for all these years. Fundamentally, I think you're two awfully nice people. Actually, you've been horribly misguided in your behavior. You're awfully emphatic in your statements, and that means you respect people who are emphatic in their statements."

B: That's a good line.

E: "You have shouted at your wife to shut up, and she's shouted at you to shut up. I don't see why I should be the only polite one in this office. I don't see why I can't follow your example and tell you to shut up when there's good reason for you to shut up." He is going to agree with me. But he is thereby committing himself that when I do tell him to shut up, there's a good reason.

H: Do you ever, with a family, push the family into an alliance against you to bring about some incident?

E: Oh yes.

H: We can use an example of that. (Laughter)

E: I've done that recently. I angered the husband and wife against me. I can't think of what it was. Oh yes. I angered the husband and I angered the wife. I just got a letter from the husband. I got a verbal relay through a friend of the wife. I antagonized both of them against me. They'd come out to Phoenix to see me, and they spent the agreed-upon time there. I angered them very, very much. Because otherwise they wouldn't take therapy. The wife insisted on having her mother visit. The husband couldn't stand the old lady, and I don't blame him one bit. The only reason his wife endured her mother was because her husband could tolerate her mother even less. The husband was getting even with his wife by having one big car for him, one big car for her, and he had three of these foreign-made cars, small, foreign-made cars. He couldn't possibly afford five cars for the two of them to drive. They had so much indebtedness. I got both of them mad at me, and they went back home furious at me. They left without saying goodbye, and all the way home on the plane confided in each other how mad they were at me. The husband very carefully sold his big car and two of the foreign-made cars, because he only needed one small foreign-made car. His wife didn't like to drive the foreign cars. He used that money to clean up some of the indebtedness. His wife was so relieved; and she didn't want me to be right, because I had antagonized her by accusing her of just slapping her husband across the face with that damn mother of hers. I accused the husband of slapping his wife across the face with those damn cars of his. They proceeded to prove me wrong. Now the husband has written to me telling me all about disposing of the cars, and saying that I was right. His wife sent, through a friend of hers who knows me, the verbal statement that I was right. It's such a relief not to have her mother visiting every day. She and her husband are getting along very nicely. He used to burn up every time he came home from the office, seeing his mother-in-law's car there. He's a doctor. His wife would burn up every time she'd go out in the yard and see those three foreign-made cars, or two of them and the big car, sitting there useless. So now I've got two friends. The only one that is problematic is the mother-in-law. But you know, even if you do make the people angry at you, after a while they will begin to recognize that they have been benefited very greatly. Whenever I use anger to benefit a patient, I tell them, very simply, "You know the thing I'm really interested in is helping you. I really don't care whether you like me or dislike me, so long as I can help you. Because you didn't come here just to make a friend out of me. You've got a lot of friends who've tried to help you, and they haven't succeeded. I'm not just going to be another friend, I want to help you. Of course, if I can be your friend and still help you, that's all right too. It's even better."

H: I think what we're concerned about is the way you can sometimes antagonize a family so that they turn against you and gloss over the really basic differences between them, and they stick together when they shouldn't really.

E: But you don't want that to happen.

H: No. This is why I was interested in whether you made them angry or not and how you did it.

* * *

E: This matter of rigidity of people – two clinical psychologists came to me one year at Wayne County General Hospital. Man and wife. One sent from one college, and one sent from another, for an internship in clinical psychology. They arrived together, and I was utterly horrified that Yale would send men like that, and that – I think it was Smith – would send me a girl like that. Two of the most rigid, inhibited, prudish, prim people I never want to see again. So rigid. They came in and it didn't take long to get their history. They both came from New England families – rigid and prim and prudish, only children. They had met because their families thought that the other came from the right kind of family. Everything of that sort. The fact she had gone to Smith College hadn't done the girl any good in the correction of her attitudes. Yale hadn't done anything for the man. Betty was in the hospital having a baby, so I invited the two to have lunch with me. I cooked them lunch. I took them in the basement kitchen of ours at Eloise, and I slid a couple chairs out across the kitchen floor for them to sit in. We had lots of dishes in that kitchen there. Various sets of dishes were stored in our cupboards. I set the table. I had three different kinds of plates. I had mismatched cups and saucers. I put the milk on the table in the bottle. I fried some pork chops. We had a dog named OT trained to lie in the corner of the breakfast room. I cooked that dinner. I warmed up some cold potatoes, I've forgotten what all. I had glasses for their milk of different sizes. Mismated everything at the table. All the silverware was mismated. I brought the pork chops heated in the skillet, and I brought the warmed-up potatoes in the skillet. I had the bread there. They were used to a butler and a maid, and things like that. So I took my fork and I dished out their pork chops. I scraped the potatoes out of the skillet onto their plates with my fork, and then I helped myself. Then I took my fork and speared a slice of bread and tossed it gently. And I poured some milk for them. I had coffee for myself. They kept up a running fire of conversation.

B: That you kept up.

E: Oh yes. On clinical psychology, opportunities for study at Eloise, and so on. I picked up my pork chop in my hand, and I ate it. Then when I finished I dropped it over my shoulder on the terrazzo floor. The dog very gladly got up and came over and cleaned up the grease spot, ate the bone, and went back to the corner. Then I speared another. After licking my fork I speared another pork chop. When we ran out of pork chops, I picked up another fork, hesitated, recognized that it was a clean fork, speared a pork chop, some more bread, some more potatoes. I tossed my second bone over my shoulder and OT ate it. That's the dog. Then I poured me a glass of milk, while I was still talking interestedly, and I tipped that glass of milk slowly over onto the floor. By that time they both said, "Oh don't, Dr. Erickson, don't Dr. Erickson, don't." The idea of pouring milk on the floor. Of course, the dog came over and licked it up. I said, "You're both about ready to faint; you just can't take it anymore." The girl said, "No, I was trained you never put food on the floor; you're just about making me cry, I can't stand it." Then I turned to her husband. I said, "How do you feel?" He said, "I feel exactly the same way as my wife does, this has been the most miserable meal. I hate to say it but the behavior has been perfectly outrageous." I said, "That's right. Now really, do you expect to do a Rorschach examination, a thematic apperception test, an intelligence test, with a psychotic patient and expect Emily Post behavior? Or are you going to go into a state of panic when a patient says something slightly out of the way to you? You've just about passed out because I poured a little milk on the floor, because I threw bones on the floor. The dog cleaned them up, you can see the floor is perfectly clean. You almost passed out because you thought the plates and cups and saucers should match. You want things in perfect order, and you're not going to get things in perfect order on the ward. What do you think about it?" They said, "We have been discussing that and we've been rather alarmed." They said, "All the way here we wondered how we would deal with patients." But after that introduction, the girl went to the ward. She came back rather shaken because I introduced her to the worst possible patient, as I did the man, to the worst possible female patient. At the end of the summer there wasn't anything you could say to them that could cause them to bat an eyelash.

But that rigidity that people have that's so built in. You tell the patient that comes to you with this rigidity, whether it's a family interview or not, there are some things that have to be discussed. Things that have to be called by name. I can give you the example of a bride and groom who came to me after less than a month of married life. The bride insisted on seeing me. The groom said his mind was made up; he was going to get a divorce. He could not tolerate the outrageous behavior of his bride. He expressed, rather emphatically, an unfavorable opinion of psychiatrists. Finally I said, "Now you've expressed your opinion and I'm going to speak with equal frankness. You've been married less than a month, and you're talking about a divorce. I don't know what kind of a coward you are, but you ought to see at least one month of your marriage through to the bitter end. So kindly shut up and listen to what your bride has to say to me." He did just that – he folded his arms and set his jaw and listened. His bride said, "Henry doesn't believe in making love in the right fashion. He wants all the lights off, he wants the curtains drawn, and he wants to undress in the privacy of the bathroom. He won't enter the bedroom unless the lights are completely off. I'm supposed to wear my nightie and not take it off. All he wants to do is have sex relations in the most simple fashion possible. He won't even kiss me." I asked him, "Is that right?" and he said, "I believe in having sex relations in the proper manner without getting maudlin over it." She continued, "He just seems to avoid touching me. He won't kiss my breasts or play with them. He won't even touch them." The husband responded, "Breasts are utilitarian; they are intended for infants." I told him that my inclination was to sympathize with his wife, and he probably wouldn't like what I had to say. "Therefore," I said, "you sit there and keep your arms folded and your jaw clenched. Be as angry as you wish, because I'm going to tell your wife some of the things I think she ought to know."

So I told the bride in what fashion I thought her husband ought to kiss her breasts and nurse her nipples. I pointed out how he ought to kiss her and where he ought to kiss her, and he should enjoy it. As a healthy female, she should enjoy it. Then I pointed out that human beings have an anthropomorphic tendency. They name their guns "Old Betsy," their boats "Stay-Up," and their cabins "Do-Come-In." They have any number of pet names for possessions of various kinds. I said I thought her husband, since he said he loved her, ought to have some pet names for her twins. She looked a little baffled, and I said, "You know they *are* twins." and I indicated her breasts. The twins really ought to have names that rhymed, I said, and I turned to the young man and put the matter to him firmly. I said, "Now tomorrow at your next interview, you will come in with twin names for your wife's breasts. If you don't name them, I will name one of them, and you will be stuck with the name of the other, which will come to your mind immediately." He stalked out of the office.

The next day they came in, and the wife said, "Well, Henry has tried to make love in a much better fashion. He seems to have more understanding, but he says he's never going to name the twins." I turned to him and said, "Are you going to name the twins? Remember, if you're unwilling to do it, I'll name one with a rhyming name, and you will be stuck with the name of the other." He said, "I'm not going to be undignified about my wife's breasts." I suggested that he might want to think it over for half an hour while we took up some of the other questions. So we discussed other aspects of their sexual adjustment, as the wife wished. Finally, at the end of half an hour, I said to him, "Now are you ready with the names for the twins? I'm ready, but I hope you are." He said, "I just defy you." I explained again that I would name one, and the rhyming name would come to his mind immediately. When he again refused, I said to the wife, "Well, are you ready?" She said she was. I said, "I now christen your right breast 'Kitty.'" (Laughter) The bride was pleased. They were from out of state, and six months later I got a Christmas card from them. It was signed with their names and "K. and T." The wife wrote me that her husband had turned out to be a pleasing lover and took a great deal of pride and satisfaction in the twins. A couple of years later I visited their town and had dinner with a friend who knew them. He said, "What a pleasant couple they are. I remember how Henry was when they first got married, but he has really become human." Later on I got a card from them and, in addition to "K. and T." there were several other additions to the family. There's your example of aggression.

H: Pretty aggressive. (Laughter)

E: Because what on earth can he do with that name, "Kitty"? He takes a great deal of pride and satisfaction, as Ann wrote in the letter, in the twins. Often in psychotherapy you meet problems by using that neurotic compulsion in a therapeutic way. His compulsive need to avoid her breasts. I just used that compulsion in relationship to her breasts. He just wouldn't kiss her breasts. He wouldn't touch her breasts, he wouldn't play with them with his hands. He said they were utilitarian and they were intended for infants.

H: Well now, how do you connect this? You used it – I'm not following you here for a moment. You used his avoidance.

E: His avoidance, his compulsive avoidance, but I made the entire thing compulsive in another way.

H: You mean a compulsive rhyme?

E: A compulsive rhyme. And kitty, that's an affectionate. Titty, that's an affectionate, and there's no escaping it.

W: Not in that context.

E: No. There's no escaping it. So all that compulsion became centered around an affectionate – what would you call it – an affectionate naming of the breast. He had to think about Miss Kitty and Titty. Kitty and

Titty. And Kitty is such a nice term. So his compulsion was just reversed.

H: That's the tricky thing, the reversal you put on compulsion. If they're going to be compulsive, you might as well compel them in the right direction. That seems to be your approach.

E: Yes. Ann says that Joe turned out to be a very pleasing lover. He really discovered what a titty was for. (Laughter)

H: You have an odd way of taking the usual clinical diagnostic categories and somehow using them as an approach to the patient. I imagine with phobias, since it's avoiding something phobically, you'd get them avoiding the right thing in the same sort of a way.

E: You use the phobia. The patient's got a lot of strength and force built into that phobia, and therefore you use that.

* * *

H: One of the things I would like to discuss is a typical kind of couple where the wife is overwhelming her husband and wishing she couldn't. Where the husband is – I don't know quite how to phrase it – the husband does something, the wife objects or in some way puts him down, and instead of overcoming her in this kind of a struggle, he steps down. She continually puts him in his place, and she doesn't want to really. You get this difficulty either in a sexual sphere or in just any kind of argument.

W: In a case where she sort of challenges him, instead of taking it as a challenge he collapses instead of coming up to it.

H: You can put it as testing. She's testing him all the time to see if he's really the boss, and continually he doesn't meet the test. Several of our couples and families are this way.

W: It could be seen as a statement, "Don't push me around," where it actually is a statement, "Are you a man or not?" He doesn't respond like a man, he responds like, "Yes dear, I won't shove you too hard."

H: The couples I see in my practice too, this is a typical problem between them, or it's certainly a manifestation of the problem between them.

E: I can think of a couple that I handled in *this* way. The wife liked to go out to dinner. She enjoyed going out to dinner, and her husband enjoyed taking her. But it was always a farce, it worked out that way. He would agree to take her any place that she wanted to go, and in looking at the menu, he would say, "You would like this, wouldn't you?" He always chose her food. "Would you like your steak well done?" Of course, she wanted it rare, but how could she when that sweet husband so thoughtfully and considerately ordered things for her? He always picked the restaurants and the table, and he always asked the orchestra to play special pieces for her. He selected the pieces for her without consulting her. It always worked out that she never got the food she wanted. They never went to the restaurant she wanted to go to. She always had to admit that it was a nice dinner, a nice restaurant, the orchestra was very nice, everything was wonderful; and she would go home and be full of fury and rage and helpless. He would always add, "You tell me if you have any other choice. Well now, let's see the next restaurant that you would like." So he always gave her an opportunity to correct him verbally, but no time in which to correct him. So utterly sweet.

H: I think this is another problem, but it's a very pertinent one. It's another one that we run into all the time.

E: Therefore, in a joint interview with them, he said he didn't believe he did a thing like that. He certainly wouldn't. He didn't believe he did it that way. He certainly wouldn't want to do it that way, and he explained it to his wife until she finally agreed, in my presence, that he didn't do it that way. Then she said, "You see what I mean?" (Laughter) And he looked just as blank as he could be. So I asked him if he would be willing to take his wife out to dinner with his wife asking him to drive down a certain street and surprising him with the restaurant. Actually, what I did was I listed–took a city map and I began listing the streets that he would drive down. So many blocks, and at 2200 he would turn right, drive eight blocks, turn left and go nine or ten blocks. I had him literally circle around the city. Here and there, turning right, turning left, going east, going west, going north, going south, until it was the most bewildering sort of thing. As they drove, his wife read the directions. (Laughter) Until finally she said, "Now the next instruction is to turn right at the first restaurant. So they went into the Blue Grotto restaurant. I had that elaborate pathway all worked out, and her husband by that time was so thoroughly in a receiving state of mind. (Laughter) She said, "Now it says here on the paper we enter the Blue Grotto, we walk past the first two booths, then we walk past the table on the righthand side, and then we walk over toward the row of booths, then we walk around another table." So they just followed that. He followed along. The waitress came in and brought them menus. She looked at the paper and she said, "Now we'll trade menus." (Laughter) They read the menus, he said, "Shall I give the order, dear?" She said, "Yes, I'll just trade menus." Now he got the menu that *she* had been reading, and *she* got the menu on which *he* had made the selections. Unwittingly, when the waitress took the order, he was looking at *her* menu. I told her to say, "Yes, that's my menu." He said, "What would you like?" Because she had the menu from which the choice had been made. Do you see that? They had identical menus, but he had studied the menu and held it in his hand. She told him that she wanted a filet mignon, let's say, medium rare, and a chef's salad with Roquefort dressing. So she selected each item from the menu which he had looked at. She gave the wrong orders, of course. But she held in her hand that particular menu. "I want you to select anything on the menu," but this was hers. He kept looking at *his* menu and closing it and asking her.

W: It's almost as if he had actually marked the menu and then handed it to the wife.

E: That's right. He was an orderly, meticulous man. (Laughter) You see, that first trading of the menus, well that was *his* menu, the one from which he had made the choice. He marked it and then, all of a sudden, it got into his wife's hands. He's such an utterly, completely meticulous man. That's why he carried such a list.

B: How do you know what order of judgment is involved in saying that he would, therefore, be meticulous with the second menu that he receives? Suppose with the first change of menu he has already said, "This menu that I first had is *my* menu without change, now it's come back to me."

E: My instruction to Evelyn was, "As soon as a waitress gives you a menu, you pick it up. She'll undoubtedly give him his menu second. Now you watch very carefully, don't open yours, as soon as he picks his up – change. Before he's got a chance, but you've taken his menu away. Therefore he's got to abide by your choice."

B: Had she chosen the restaurant or did you?

E: Oh I chose it. You see I took the city map and mapped out this criss-cross back and forth.

B: But he didn't know that you had chosen the restaurant?

E: She had mentioned that she would like to go to this restaurant, that one, and she hadn't been to the Blue Grotto, among a number of others, because he tended to go regularly to about five particular restaurants.

W: Well, among the things you've done there, to start off with, is to set up a program—this turn left, four blocks, turn right, even more meticulous than his, but which is obviously stupid as a means of getting somewhere.

E: Yes. Because actually the Blue Grotto was almost on a straight line from where they lived. (Laughter) Going north and south, east and west, and finally winding up on the west side of town, almost in a straight line.

B: Did he arrive at the restaurant in a rage?

E: He was amused, and he was thinking about how nicely those directions worked out so well that he would arrive at the Blue Grotto. It's a work of art from his point of view. He was very meticulous. (Laughter)

H: Now you had her read *your* directions, and he would follow the directions because they came from you; but by the fact that she was reading them, that made them come from her?

E: That's right.

H: This is another alliance situation?

E: Another alliance.

H: Well now, what did this do in the way of setting it up so that the next time they spontaneously went out to dinner with a different arrangement?

E: The next time they went out to dinner, hubby looked over the situation and he said, "We had such a delightful time at the Blue Grotto, driving in that absurd, ridiculous way. Let's drive the same sort of a way and see what sort of a restaurant we wind up at." So he literally repeated that 17 blocks west, 10 blocks south, 18 blocks east, 7 blocks north, until finally they'd driven at random, hither and yon. Finally he said, "Now after we drive 10 blocks more, let's stop at the first good-looking restaurant we see." So then they were at liberty to pick the first good-looking restaurant they saw.

H: So this became not a choice that would deprive her but kind of a random choice?

E: It would be a random choice of the first good-looking restaurant that they saw. And of course he was driving. I've forgotten which restaurant it was. If I remember correctly, it was a Chinese restaurant on East Thomas. She said, "That looks like a nice place, turn in." He was trying to take charge by following that original pattern I had given them of taking her instruction. Taking charge while taking her instructions. It was a new place. He had no patterns set up, and his wife immediately announced her wishes. She was following the pattern of the Blue Grotto.

H: You seem to feel if you can get them to change their pattern once, the next time they'll also do it. They won't fall back on the previous one.

E: Oh, to prevent that I said, "Now you're going out to dinner a number of times more before Christmas. There are at least five places that you will not go," and I named the ones they usually went to.

H: You cut off the previous ones.

E: I cut off the ritualistic selections of the past.

H: Why would you do it in terms of switching menus, rather than more directly in terms that she was to make the choice?

E: Say that again.

H: Why didn't you just instruct her to make the choice of what they would have for dinner?

E: Because he was one of those meticulous guys that took the menu and read it very carefully. He examined that menu from the uppermost line on, right straight down. He had read everything on the menu before he ordered – systematically.

W: Well, Milton covers more ground this way. He does something not only for her situation with the husband, but also about the husband's meticulousness, as I see it.

E: Yes. And I knew from her descriptions how he would examine the menu.

H: You don't interpret or comment on what a difficult position he puts her in by being so sweet and benevolent?

E: He couldn't understand that. But that Blue Grotto dinner was one of the nicest dinners he and she ever had. She really enjoyed it, and she went all out in telling him so. That was the first time he had ever experienced that sort of gratitude. He used to buy her flowers, very thoughtfully, for the weekend. There would be a table piece, centerpiece, of flowers, which always threw her into a silent fury. He never managed to get her the flowers she liked. It was always a completely ornate centerpiece for the table. I had him go down to one of those newsstands and ask a newsstand operator, "Have you got a yesterday's paper, or have you got some out-of-town paper that's left over?" He bought that to take to a florist. He told the florist, "I'm playing a joke on somebody. I'd like some nice flowers. Whatever you think would be a nice joke on somebody, a very nice joke. So I'll put the flowers in this paper, just wrap it up and I'll present it to them." So he walked into the house, and his wife wondered what centerpiece he'd bring home that weekend. He handed her this out-of-town newspaper. She was horribly puzzled. Those flowers she received were a florist's choice, and a practical joke. What did the florist do? He put in roses, and he put in pansies, and various flowers that didn't seem to fit together and match. It was no effort at an elaborate arrangement. His wife, of course, got this completely disarranged bunch of flowers. The exact opposite of an ornate center-of-the-table piece. Her husband discovered again that he could present something to his wife that pleased her immeasurably.

H: Well now, apparently you assume that his previous choices were just a lack of understanding of what his wife wanted.

E: He was raised in the East in absolute formality. She grew up on a farm.

H: Now if he consistently brought her what she didn't want, this was a sign of some resentment more than just a choice of his because of a lack of understanding.

E: It was a lack of understanding with her, because he couldn't possibly conceive of how anybody would want anything else. That absolute rigidity. Their wedding anniversaries were always celebrated with pomp and circumstance. She told me how she anticipated their sixth wedding anniversary. "We'll have a private dining room. We'll have the waiters, we'll have an ornate cake. We'll have all the proper people there; all the proper toasts will be made, the right champagne. We'll have a babysitter there the night before. We'll take a suite in the hotel in preparation for our sixth anniversary." So I told him, "Your wedding anniversary's coming up. It would be very, very delightful to surprise your wife. Give her a surprise that is absolutely unforgettable." So I outlined for him a surprise for her. He looked at me in absolute horror. (Laughter) I said, "Go to your sister-in-law. I'll call her up in advance. She will give you the full instructions. I want you to rent a pick-up truck. Go to the store and buy sleeping bags and tents, and camping equipment. Buy bacon and eggs and hot dogs and hamburgers. Buy your wife Levis and your sister-in-law knows the size. She has the same size feet. Get her rough shoes. Then you drive into the yard tomorrow afternoon at four o'clock. Tell your wife, 'Here's your clothes, put them on. You've got a surprise coming.' Take her out to the desert for a wedding anniversary breakfast before going camping out. After a night's sleep, you can really do a little mountain climbing. Somewhere around noon, cook another meal, and then get in the truck and get lost." (Laughter) By that time he was in the spirit of things. He got in the truck and he said, "I don't know where this road goes, but we're driving down it." Instead of returning to Phoenix, they wound up in Yuma. They had a very delightful time there, and then drove back. Absolutely marvelous time. Now he was in to see me the other day, and they've been camping on weekends all this past summer. They thoroughly enjoy it. She grew up on a farm. She and her siblings had gone camping. They had gone to Sunday school picnics. They'd gone to Girl Scout camps, and camping out overnight. He grew up in a wealthy New England family. There was a butler and a maid, the upstairs maid and the downstairs maid, and the basement maid and the cook, who did everything. He did what Emily Post said was proper. Now he has become a decidedly different sort of person. He looks me up about three times a year to review his adjustments and his wife's adjustments. She comes in here about twice a year just to review things.

W: Well now, we have the picture here that sort of highlighted him. I wonder if there's anything you might say about – did she take a part in this picture or was it all, so to speak, his doing?

E: She grew up as a nice farm girl in a nice, solid, substantial family. Then her father struck it rich. He got social climbing ideas, and his wife had social climbing ideas. That's what led to her acquaintance with this man. Her parents really approved. He's a nice guy. Her marriage occurred before she really knew what the situation was, and she was caught in it. Since she was such a nice, sweet, farm country girl, she didn't know how to deal with the situation. But once she learned a little bit, then her husband tried to take it over; but he had to take it over in a peculiar pattern that I had created for him, which gave his wife a lot to say about it.

W: I'm still wondering if, in addition to his benevolence, perhaps she wasn't so sweet, that she was a little bit caught up in the same thing. She was going along with it sweetly, in a way that sort of reinforced his . . .

E: She didn't know how to deal with it. She felt so helpless, and yet she knew her wants. But you see that change her father and mother all of a sudden imposed upon her after the age of 18 when father struck it rich.

H: I think you tend, Milton, to interpret people's being mean to one another as a lack of understanding.

E: There usually is. (Laughter) He was not really mean to her; it worked out that way. She wasn't really mean to him, but it worked out that way. She never did have proper gratitude.

H: Well if she, over a period of time, never expressed proper gratitude, and never felt proper gratitude, and he over this period of time never received this gratitude, there's a pretty powerful resentful feeling building up.

E: Oh yes.

H: This isn't what you deal with. You deal with the lack of understanding rather than the resentment.

E: Yes. Their sexual behavior was pretty terrible. She was cold toward him. He had premature ejaculations. She would get sexually hungry; he would have his premature ejaculation. Then when he did control his ejaculation, that was the time she was definitely not interested in sex and would unwillingly submit. And yawn during intercourse. (Laughter) So it was a pretty unpleasant thing. Socially he was so terribly polite, but whenever they went out to the country club, he would be so polite to somebody that unpleasant things would develop that would embarrass her.

H: Well other schools of therapy would encourage them to express their resentment toward each other in verbal ways. Talk about how they resented what each other was doing and go through that, and then work into something better, and you just by-pass it I gather?

E: I bypass it. If the house is uncleanable, move out. (Laughter) Because the important thing is to live in a pretty house. If the house is uncleanable, move out.

H: Well, a different sort of a problem – the problem of the husband and wife, where they go out to dinner and the wife has to initiate going out to dinner, and when they get there she selects what food to have. There's always some resentment, on her part, of the fact that she has to do the initiating of everything; and at the same time if her husband does more initiating where to go, she objects. It's sort of a reversal of what you're talking about. Where the wife is in charge and the husband isn't.

W: If you decide to bring the husband up some, what reactions would there be on the other side?

E: Quite often I've told a dominant woman, in very complimentary terms, my appreciation of her competency. Then I raise the questioning doubt – my inability to understand a woman of her intelligence neglecting to use the competencies of her husband. One of the things I do in that connection is this: I point out that biologically a man is quite another order of creature than is the female. His entire philosophy of life is different, his whole psychological functioning is different in relationship to children. It's the mother who's one completed sexual act takes about 16 years to complete. That includes receiving the sperm, carrying the unborn child, nine months of gestation, the lactation. It requires all of the physiological changes in the body, all of the physical changes in the body, all of the transformations of the body that occur in the woman. That it includes taking care of the baby, teaching it, nurturing it, educating it, and guiding it and protecting it through long years of childhood, and that biologically a woman is so oriented. When my dominant woman listens to that, she has a legitimate excuse for her dominance. But as surely as she accepts that legitimate excuse for dominance, then she lays herself open to the responsibility of utilizing every favorable influence in the environment. Now among the favorable influences in the environment is this husband of hers who represents another order of biological experience. Another order of biological learning. And since her child will have to live in a world of men *and* women and must deal with both, and since her child is either a man or a woman, there must be an adequate awareness of the biological character and structure of the self, and the biological character and the structure of the opposite sex. The dominant woman is literally made to recognize that she better utilize those innate, inherent things in the biological structure of her husband.

W: Have you another example where a woman insists on being in charge and then resents her husband because he's not in charge?

E: I can think of the husband and wife who went into business running a restaurant. She wanted him to manage that restaurant, and she pointed out to him that he should manage that restaurant. But, as he stated, "Yes, now she tells me that I should run that restaurant. I'm the busboy, I'm the janitor. I scrub the floors, and she nags at me because I don't do the buying. She nags at me because I don't do the bookkeeping. She nags at me because I don't run the business. She runs it. But she points out to me that the floor needs scrubbing. I really ought to get someone to scrub the floor, but I can't wait until somebody comes in and asks for the job, so I wind up doing it myself. Then there's no need of hiring someone to do it."

That's how the situation was. The question was, how would I handle that? The wife had no insight into the situation at all. She said, yes, she did want him to be the man that ran that restaurant. She wanted to be at home. She had some sewing to do, she wanted her husband to have something more than restaurant cooking. She wanted to do her own home cooking. He had to eat at least one meal at the restaurant, but why not have a home cooked meal instead of that restaurant cooking? Why not cook the very special foods with the special seasonings that he liked. That was her insistence. And her husband's statement was, "Yes, that's what she says; you can hear it, I can hear it. She'll be in the restaurant tomorrow morning." So what I did with her was to raise the question of who carried the keys to the restaurant? Who locked up? It was somewhere around 10 or 10:30, 11 o'clock, that he went home; and he opened in the morning for the breakfast trade. Who ought to carry the keys? She said, "We both carry the keys. I always get there first. He's parking the car." So I pointed out to her that she ought to see to it that her husband gets there one-half hour before she does. That was where the break came. He carried the keys, and he opened the door, and unlocked everything. All the details of starting up a restaurant. I had him list all the things he took charge of in that one-half hour. His wife arrived a half an hour late. She didn't quite see the sense in arriving a half an hour late. They had only one car. But I pointed out to them that their home was only a few blocks from the restaurant. If she wanted to, she could drive her husband to the restaurant, or he could walk. But she arrived at the restaurant completely out of step and way behind. One-half hour behind him. There had been so many things that he had already set into motion. He was managing then, do you see that?

H: I see that as a breakthrough, but not entirely a solution.

E: Once she yielded on that half hour in the morning, then she yielded on going home at 6 o'clock. That put another break in the day.

H: Well, there is another side to this sort of a relationship that we see, and that is the husband inviting his wife to take charge; while protesting that she's always taking charge, he's also inviting her.

E: He's inviting her, that's right. Now I didn't point out to the husband, "Yes, you end up mopping the floor when your wife wants you to because you invite her to tell you to mop the floor. You invite her to tell you to scrub out the garbage cans." Because he wouldn't have understood that. But he did begin to understand that he was in charge for a whole half hour. That was what he *could* understand. He was a perfectly competent man.

W: Well, from what I've seen of families, that might take a very critical amount of arranging by you simply to insure that he's going to get there that half hour early, and that she is going to get there a half hour later. I wonder how you really nailed that down, because I've seen them be awfully slippery on making any definite change like that whatsoever. What I got was that you ask her to see to it that he got there a half hour ahead of her.

E: That was *her* management. (Laughter) Asking her to manage to defeat herself.

W: She doesn't see that this is happening; she sees similarities but not the difference?

E: Not the difference. Of course, that left her with the breakfast dishes and the housework. She could be half an hour late – you know, she could be 35 minutes late. That was another thing she didn't recognize. In fact, she could be 40 minutes late. She could be an hour late. Thereby she was discovering that her husband could get along without her. Her husband was at the same time discovering that he could manage the restaurant. His wife was discovering the management of their home, the importance of her other activities. It finally wound up that she ran the cashier's desk during the cashier's vacations. In case of sickness of an employee, when they were rushed, she would drop in.

I can think of another restaurant couple. Every day his wife went down to check to see if he was running that restaurant correctly. He was utterly furious about it. Yet he let her do it. He recited his lessons each day. She spent about two hours there checking up on everything. She'd drop in 1 o'clock, 2 o'clock, 3 o'clock in the afternoon. He was utterly furious; but he'd recite his lessons, recite his reports. I asked her about that, and she said she couldn't resist that need to dominate her husband. What did she want to do about it? She said she'd do anything in the world to get over it. So I gave her the task of reporting to her husband. Now you quiz him thoroughly on every point. You've got a list of the questions you always ask. Then I want you to frame parallel questions concerning *your* day's activities. She framed the questions, and she quizzed her husband, and then she answered for her husband her own questions about her activity. Her husband was still being quizzed, but it always wound up with her being in her husband's role except that she was managing it by literally asking her own questions of herself in reporting to her husband. She had complete management. And you know, she got so fed up with that. I took all of the pleasure out of dominating her husband.

H: She handed him the list to ask, is that it?

E: Oh no. She made out a list for me of the questions she always asked her husband.

H: Yes.

E: Then I had her make out a comparable list that her husband could ask her.

H: Well then, she gave him this list to ask?

E: Oh no. And I told her to keep that list. You don't have to refer to it to quiz your husband. But after you are through quizzing your husband, you look at this list that you keep in your handbag, and then you tell him, I have done this.

H: Without his asking?

E: Without his asking. You see, I put the management completely in her hands. But forced her to put herself into a . . . how do you pronounce that word . . . recitative role.

W: But here that makes it even more so, when you get her to put herself in that position somehow.

E: The last time I talked to them, oh, it was over a year

ago, the only time she ever goes to that restaurant is when she drops in with some one of her social friends and orders something. She never reports on the household. She runs that. And they built a new house, an expensive house, and she's running that to his complete satisfaction. He has been in the restaurant business, let's see, he is in his 50s – he started out as a high school kid interested in restauranting. He had his first hot dog, hamburger stand in his early 20s. He had a restaurant in Chicago; his son got asthma, they moved to Phoenix. After all the years in Chicago, even when she was dating him, she asked him his daily catechism on the running of his restaurant, before they were even married. So he invited that trouble.

W: One thing different in this is that she had some recognition of what she was doing.

E: But felt compelled to do it.

W: That's different from the other couple.

E: You see, she recognized it and felt compelled and so helpless about it. Therefore, I utilized that feeling of compulsion by letting her apply it to herself.

W: You got her to compel herself with that other list.

E: Compel herself with the other list, and that altered the character of the compulsion. How is your stock of this, and how is your stock of that? Her statement to him – I ordered a seven-course meal for the household. I bought two loaves of bread. The family is going to have roast beef.

H: It seems so simple now. You have a way of looking at what's going on. It seems obvious when you explain it; yet when someone tries to apply it to a couple or a family, it isn't quite so obvious.

W: No, if we'd seen that restaurant couple, this might not have leaped to the eye.

H: Yes.

E: Yes, but you see, so often the tendency is to look at one specific aspect of the central complaint of a husband and wife. Now there are a lot of other things between the husband and wife. That restaurant was his entire life, and she was really interested in her husband. She didn't know how to manifest it.

H: Let me pose a situation, for example: You're seeing a husband and wife. The wife had anxiety attacks which she is now over. But they have a relationship where she is constantly protesting how inadequate the guy is. He doesn't initiate anything. She has to initiate going out. She has to suggest this and that. He goes along with whatever she recommends. It reaches the extreme that when she does housework on Saturday morning, he follows her. He just walks around and watches her do housework, making her very uncomfortable. Now she's not happy with this situation. But they get in terrific arguments when he does suggest doing something, or when he does take a little more assertive role in the marriage. Now this is the situation; it's an obvious situation, and it isn't obvious what to do about it.

E: Well, what else is there about them?

H: Well, it's two college graduates, both of them feeling absolutely inadequate about getting a good job. He works on a magazine. She was working as a typist for two years, and then she had her anxiety attack and quit. She's now gone back to work there. That's the only job in the world she could have, and the only job she could look for. She'd be afraid to look for a job anywhere else except at the University in the same department where she'd been working before. So now they both work. She's afraid to have children, afraid to have babies; this will kill her, she'll have a heart attack or something of the sort. He is working on a magazine. He's a journalism graduate. He isn't happy with the job. He'd like to be a writer, sort of, vaguely. They just live. They have very few friends. They have very little social life because they're uncomfortable in groups.

E: Do they save any money?

H: They are beginning to save a little now. They were awfully broke for a period because she wasn't working and he was making a small salary. They're vaguely saving for a down payment for a house.

E: And he follows her around, watches her sweep this room, and then follows her into the other room and watches her sweep that room. Which one do you want to make mad at the other?

H: I don't want to make either one of them mad; I want to make them a little happy.

E: Yes. But so far, given what you describe to me, it seems to me what I would do in that situation is to cast around for some way of making one of them mad at the other in a rather unnecessary way. That is, now suppose I could generate a fight between you and Gregory on the subject of, "Should you put a campfire on the west side of this brook or on the east side of the brook?" How often are you going to be at that brook? Not very often. Build up a situation where you can generate a quarrel in a situation that is not likely to occur again. Neither wants to quarrel with the other. Both are going to have, if you can generate a good quarrel, an increased emotional respect for the other. And they never notice what you're doing to them.

H: Well, they can quarrel, but they'll quarrel on the fact that he didn't lock the door when they left.

E: I know.

H: Or he didn't do this, or he didn't do that.

E: Yes. On inadequate things. On stupid, feeble little things. Why not a good fight? A good fight, and an intense fight?

W: But about something that's limited so that they won't go on.

E: That's right. I would try to make this following her—I'd get the details from her, so I'd know how to utilize it. He follows her from room to room as she sweeps the floor. I would really want to penalize him horribly. But I'd want to penalize *her* at the same time. I'd build up the situation with her. "Just see to it that he follows you through the living room, the dining room, the kitchen, the hallway; and sweep the floor very carefully and let him watch you. And keep attracting his attention. Say, 'I'm sweeping up this corner.' After you've got the floor all swept, go and get that bag that you've got prepared in the kitchen. Start where you began the sweeping, and take a little handful of leaves and dirt and grass and put it there. Go through all the rooms, see to it he follows you through. Then tell him, 'You know, next Saturday I'm going to sweep the floor again.'" Now, what will that do to her and what will that do to him?

H: I don't know, what will it do?

E: Here's an impossible situation. You've got to do something about it. You can't sweep the floor until next Saturday.

H: She would be instructed not to sweep it until next Saturday?

E: Until next Saturday.

H: This would be discussed with her alone?

E: Yes, and you do not discuss the matter.

H: She is not to discuss it with him when he says, "For God's sake, we can't leave this on the floor all week?"

E: That's right.

B: The floor has not been particularly prepared.

H: The floor has just been swept with him following her, she then takes a bag of crap and goes around and sprinkles the crap afterward. Then she says, "I'll have to sweep the floor again next Saturday."

E: I've discussed with her what she's to do. So he is to follow her from room to room and observe uncritically, that is, verbally, vocally uncritically; and after she finishes messing up the floor, she says, "I will have to sweep the floor a week from now, next Saturday." They would both know that I had specified no discussion. They've got a week's time in which to deal with a major problem. It's an impossible situation.

I can give you another kind of example of that. One of my patients said, "I just can't stand it, what my neighbor does to me. Every time I mow the yard, front or back, he comes up and follows right behind me. He hasn't got much to say, he just watches me. And he's horribly troublesome. I don't like him and he doesn't like me, and he's annoying the hell out of me. I can't afford to sell my home and move to another part of town. I'm just going wild, and my wife is quarreling with his wife. His way of getting even with me, his wife's way of getting even, is to have him follow me around. If I tell him to get out of my yard, he just stands on the edge and he watches me. He's driving me frantic. He gets home before I do, and he's sitting out there in front watching me. When I leave in the morning he's out there watching me. He's driving me batty."

I said, "Well, turnabout is fair play." What I told this man to do: "Make a collection of pieces of tire cord, pieces of board, of tin cans, wadded-up pieces of newspaper. And mow three or four swatches across the front of the yard. Go and get an old piece of board and lay it down very carefully. Mow some more of the front yard; and then in the middle of that patch, put a tin can, sit back and look at it, cramp it into place. Do the same thing in the backyard. Just ornament it, your front yard and your back yard with various things. Then go over and clip one of your flowers, say calla lilies, and take your scissors, and look at them gently. Then bend over and half break off a calla lily and leave it there."

A month later that neighbor just couldn't stand it. He wasn't out there to watch. He wouldn't watch his neighbor mow that yard. Wouldn't do anything. The man's wife wouldn't come to the back fence and say, "Your children are too noisy; isn't that tattletale grey in your clothes hanging on the line?" The neighbor just abhorred the situation. It was a completely impossible situation. In a month's time, that laborious shifting of that refuse when he mowed. That neighbor, who was set on driving him away from that neighborhood, couldn't take it.

H: Why couldn't he take it?

E: How does this work? The man's acting crazy, and he knew darn well the man *wasn't* crazy. He had committed himself to a policy of driving his neighbor crazy. The neighbor was really doing it to *him*. It doesn't make any sense to put an old piece of board, and lay it down so precisely, yet you've cut four swathes of grass, it just doesn't make sense. They have since become friends. (Laughter)

W: I realized that there's also the possible alternate on this. Suppose that this might have been, on this case, a more difficult instruction to carry out. Suppose you had had him ask his neighbor to watch him very carefully, and observe very closely what he did, so that he could really feel that if he made any mistakes, that he would have someone to check him up on it.

E: But you see, by putting that trash down, he was asking the neighbor to observe very carefully, and asking in such a way that the neighbor couldn't refuse. He was compelling the neighbor.

H: God, that's a tricky one.

E: He was asking. He was compelling, and there was no refusal possible. Any refusal of any sort would mean rejection by the neighbor of the neighbor's own pattern. And rejection by the neighbor of the neighbor's own pattern, but not at the request of my patient.

H: Not at the direct request.

E: My patient was still asking, "Give me your attention."

H: But to return to this couple again, when you set up a situation like this, which is impossible, what happens then? What are you trying to achieve with an impossible situation?

E: My patient had become interested and pleased by his own performance. He had a satisfying sense of power and pleasure. He wanted his neighbor to keep looking. He wanted a relationship with his neighbor, but it was impossible for him to foresee just what his neighbor would do. But he wanted something in relationship to his neighbor. But what that would be as a result of that peculiar behavior, he couldn't foresee; that's why they became friends eventually.

H: Well, now if I instruct this wife, who is a meticulous housekeeper, to go through this procedure: sweep the floor, pointing out how well she's sweeping the floor, and then to go around and spread this trash . . .

W: Now, does she point out how well she's doing, or does she point out just what she's doing? There's a certain difference there.

E: Well, you see I had my patient mow three swathes of grass across the front of his lawn, and then rather precisely put that scrap of old board down, and mow so much more, rather precisely put down the tin can and cramp it into place. Now with this situation, I don't know anything about the personalities. It might be the wrong thing for the people you have in mind; but you create an impossible situation, and you don't discuss it.

H: They're both instructed separately not to discuss it?

E: Yes.

H: And the husband is surprised with what happens; he isn't told what's going to happen?

E: That's right.

H: He's just told that it's not to be discussed, without being told what is not to be discussed.

E: That's right. You impress it upon him so thoroughly, and you impress it upon the wife so thoroughly.

H: So what they're faced with is a floor with trash on it, the sweeping done today, the sweeping not to be done until next Saturday, and no discussion.

E: That's right.

B: And they have the Joneses coming to dinner on Wednesday. (Laughter)

E: To get one of my aphasic patients, one that had a cerebral accident, over one of the obstacles to her improvement, I told her husband, "Listen, I want you to buy a fish tank. Make it one of those 15-gallon ones. Set it up in the den, and stock it with fish." He said, "But my wife doesn't like tropical fish." I said, "I know. You can afford that tank, and you can afford the tropical fish." Those were his instructions. I said, "Now your wife will tell you certain things to do about the fish tank. You do them. One of the things you say to your wife after you set up that fish tank, 'You talk this over with Dr. Erickson.'" So when she came in, I said, "Now your husband has purchased that fish tank, he's got it well-stocked: You hate tropical fish. You hate aquariums. All right, now I want you every night at 7 o'clock to take your husband in there and both sit there and silently watch those fish for one-half hour. You don't know why. Your husband doesn't know why. Just spend one-half hour there, and keep absolutely silent, and you tell him that he is to remain absolutely silent.

W: Which is the aphasic patient of this pair?

E: The woman. "Keep absolutely silent. At the end of the half hour – you have a clock there that you can watch – you both leave the den, and then you can resume normal living. Anything you wish." It worked out very nicely. The woman spent that half hour desperately wishing she could ask her husband, "What in hell goes on here? Why? What is Dr. Erickson trying to accomplish?" (Laughter) I wanted a tremendous motivation for talking. Her husband had told me that his wife liked to talk, but it was becoming increasingly difficult. She would just sit there and just look at him when he tried to converse with her. He couldn't understand that fish tank. If the fish tank was a diversion, look *at* the fish. Sit there silently. He wanted to talk to her, she wanted to talk to him. They could both look at each other, and they both could wish. I left them do that for about a month. You really ought to listen to that aphasic patient talk.

H: Did you forbid discussion about the tank after the half hour? No discussion of the tank at all?

E: None at all. It was an insoluble problem so far as they were concerned. With no explanation.

H: Well now, you pose apparently impossible situations, or insoluble problems, in order to require them to solve them in some different way than they have in the past, that's the idea?

E: That's right.

H: This is a Zen idea.

B: The Koan, yes.

H: The Koan.

E: He wanted his wife to talk, and she had the feeling she couldn't talk. But here's an impossible situation. Something really ought to be said about this.

B: How did you terminate? I mean, how did you end it?

E: I knew when to end it because her husband told me that his wife was really talking more and more and more freely.

B: During the day?

E: That's right. That tremendous need to talk – the knowledge that tonight I've got to go and sit there silently. (Laughter)

H: You punish her for silence. You punish her *with* silence.

E: Do you call it punishment, or do you say that you are using silence to create the motivation? You are infecting speech with values.

H: It's again what you continually do, accept what they're already doing, and have them do it on direction.

E: By the way, they both like tropical fish now. (Laughter) Sundays they are very likely to go to some of these aquariums that are open and look at fish. They can both mourn when one of the tropical fish dies – when an angel fish dies or a Maui or something of that sort.

W: And talk about it.

E: Oh yes. Now suppose I had started in the orthodox way of trying to build up her speech? This way she had no opportunity of any sort to resist building up speech. Her husband had no opportunity of antagonizing her by his insistence upon speech.

W: Well, this is very familiar to me because over the last couple of years my father, who had a stroke two or three years ago which left him weakened on the right side, has been going through a progressive process of opposition to his physical therapist. He comes home and he says, "My God, how he pushed me around today. I'm so damned tired that he knocks me out for the whole week, and he doesn't realize my situation." He progressively cuts down the number of times he goes to see him and gets himself more immobilized.

E: Yes. On the same patient, you know there's nothing sillier in the world than to try to write the name of your home town when you're right-handed but you've had a stroke on that side. Try to write the name of your home town backwards with your left hand. It's such a silly, useless thing. Why do you hold a pencil in this hand? I didn't ask her to write with her right hand, how could she avoid it? Those ancillary learnings. And she could take out all the resentment she wanted about my silly demand that she write the name of her home town with her left hand backwards. She was utterly delighted when she discovered she was writing it. Then I asked her if she could learn to write it bottom-side-up with her left hand. Upside-down yes. What did that do to the muscle control of the right arm? It's an awfully interesting task.

W: That brings in to connection other movements.

E: That's right. Now therapeutically, should I explain to her how to move this arm, and how to remember, and how to recall. Pfooey on that.

W: Well, if she's like my father, he never likes to be told anything . . .

E: But this patient, it's awfully hard for anybody to recognize that she was once aphasic, once vegetating, once horribly handicapped physically. Now I can suggest anything, no matter how utterly absurd; she'll do it.

W: Well, I take it to be a little absurd helps, doesn't it?

E: That's right because they cannot fight against absurdity. People do not have problems because they're coldly, intelligently, logically reasonable. They have problems because they *are* unreasonable and because they *are* illogical. Therefore, you meet them on their own ground.

W: On their illogical ground.

E: On the illogical ground.

CHAPTER 3

Suspicion, Joint Interviews, and Quarrels

1958. Present were Milton H. Erickson, Gregory Bateson, Jay Haley, and John Weakland.

B: What do you do with paranoid suspicion between husband and wife?

E: These paranoid suspicions?

B: Yes.

E: "Undoubtedly your husband has given you cause for suspicion. You would prefer not to be suspicious of him. You agree, do you not?"

B: "Yes."

E: "And that means that you are not going to scrutinize carefully, because you would prefer not to be suspicious, but you are, and there is reason. Don't you think it would be better if you scrutinize carefully and find out the exact reason rather than these vague, general, unwarranted reasons? Now let's see, what could be a specific reason rather than a vague, general, cloaking reason?" She will start to examine.

B: This is with husband there?

E: With the husband there. So often the answer is, "I'd rather tell you privately." You turn to the husband and state, "You know, I think it's very generous of your wife to want to tell me privately, because you know she probably has some specific reason that she wants to tell me privately. Because there is undoubtedly some doubt in her own mind." The husband is reassured, but what have I done to the wife's certainty? Because she would *like* to have a doubt you know, but I've only been talking to the husband about that doubt. I'm making it easy for the husband to leave the room. The wife knows that. I'm making it easy for her to tell this dubious suspicion. But it's going to be told as a *dubious* suspicion, though highly specific.

W: You change the meaning of privacy all around.

E: You change the meaning of the privacy. You look at the entire need for privacy. It has a wealth of possible meanings; therefore, you define it. You go out in the woods and you can camp here and here and here and here and here and here and here, and there. You look them all over, and you settle and endow this place with camping bags. Now when you actually examine it, has it got more camping values there than that place? If you'd chosen that one, you'd say it had more camping values than this place. You pick a certain tree. Is it really any better than the other trees? No. You just decide it is. That doesn't make it better. The east side or the west side of a stream? For some faulty reason you decide on the east side. But it looks like a good reason. There's a need for privacy. There's a wealth of possible interpretations for that need for privacy. So you present one that is acceptable to all concerned. Then they go along with you, and they endow it. It's your willingness to look the situation over and see the possible values of privacy. You don't limit yourself to the statement, "Well, of course you can talk more freely if your husband's out of the room." That's only one of the values.

H: When you treat an individual, inevitably, I think, you must see that their mate is involved in their problem. The question is, how do you choose, or on what basis do you choose, whether to bring the mate into it or not? Whether to treat the marriage through the individual you're working with, or whether to bring them both in?

E: Yes. You try and get a picture of the plasticity of the mate, the responsiveness of the mate. In yesterday's mail there was a letter from one of my patients. She came in to see me about preserving her marriage. As I listened to her and her description of her wishes and her hopes in regard to her husband, the more she talked about it the less hope I had of preserving the marriage. When she brought the husband in, because I had to have him come in, my judgment was correct. Because the husband explained to me so quickly and so easily – in a marriage there should be a sharing of everything. There should be a community of property. An interest, an intense interest, of the one in the other. The putting of the other's desires foremost at every possible opportunity. It was a beautiful discussion. He said when he married his wife, naturally he turned over everything he had to her, and he expected likewise. He didn't expect her to *withold*. That was an absolutely beautiful discussion – and completely meaningless. At the time he married his wife she had a son in service. He explained that when you marry you forsake all others to cling unto each other. She had a son in the service. She owned a house free and clear. She had a bank account. She had a job. What did he have? He had a perfectly beautiful car. He had a nice job. He had an ex-wife and two children. The court had ordered him to pay child support. He was $3,000 in debt for child support. He owed $1,700 on his car. He had no bank account. He wanted to put in everything he had with everything his wife had. (Laughter)

W: He put in his debts with her bank account.

E: He told it to me so simply. No matter how objectively I named the things, he couldn't possibly see the absurdity of it. He was giving his all to the common pot; she was giving her all. "You cling to each other, forsaking all others." He meant that, because your first obligation is to each other. You do not give away those things that you possess to strangers, and that son of hers was a total stranger to him. If that son came to visit his mother in the house that she now owned, he should pay for his meals and his lodging. Because why should he give to a total stranger? Now this man is a college graduate. His wife's a college graduate. That sort of pleasing discussion before marriage sounds so wonderful, so convincing. Now when I heard her describe it to me, and then found out that he wanted to charge for a meal when the son came over for a weekend visit from San Diego, right then and there I knew there was no hope for that marriage. You talk to the husband and you hear him put forth all those ideas. Yes, he's an intelligent man, but he wants his wife's bank account, he wants the house she owns put in her name and his name, and he shares his debts. She should help pay for the past child support.

W: But there are times when you only see one of a couple at all, and other times when you see them both.

E: Now it probably wasn't necessary to see that man when I heard about him charging for that meal for a weekend visit. Against her straightforward account of all her discussions. Because there you've got that violent, annihilating contrast.

Let's take Jim and Ev. Their marriage, after five years, was coming to an end. They had agreed upon a voluntary separation before they came to see me. They had nothing in common. No interests. Jim was always doing the wrong thing. Ev was never appreciative of anything. Jim was striving. Ev was striving. But they never hit upon anything of interest. They had a beautiful honeymoon. He had purchased all the tickets and made all the reservations and everything was done in advance. His wife was not a traveled person, and the wedding present from the groom to the bride was a wonderful and a complete surprise. Plane tickets to Honolulu, reservations at the Royal Hawaiian, a beautiful suite, two weeks' stay there. Absolutely complete room service for everything, a small orchestra for chamber music, valet, everything. The two weeks cost him over $5,000. He had everything that he could think of. All right, now I let him explain all of that in Ev's presence. Then I let him sit there in shocked horror when Ev told about it. They stayed in the suite for two long weeks. Everything was sent up to them. If she wanted to do any shopping, somebody brought the dresses and the jewelry and the purses and the watches up to the suite. The dresses were modeled for her in the suite. They never got out of the suite. An absolute kingdom within that suite, and she was the Royal Queen. The beauty operator came up every day, bringing apparatuses to dress her hair. Can you imagine anything as stupid as that? And he held forth on how generous he'd been. Ev said, "But I wanted to put my bare feet in the Pacific Ocean. (Laughter) I wanted to walk on the sand. I flew over the ocean. I had never seen the ocean before. We landed at the airport and there was that beautiful car that took us right to the hotel. I wanted to bend over a hibiscus bush and smell the flower myself, instead of having a maid bring in beautiful bouquets, floral arrangements from the hotel flower shop. Then we went by a special car back to the airport. Loaded on the plane, arrangements had been made so that we got a special loading."

H: So you had him describe it first and then had him listen while she described it. You say that before you bring in the mate, you first try to get an idea of the responsiveness of the mate. How do you judge when you're talking to one individual how responsive another individual is?

E: All right, now I see the mate sitting there and instead of listening to his wife and understanding, I see him mentally figuring out the rebuttal. Have you ever watched debaters? They don't listen to the argument. They are figuring out the rebuttal. What can I say that will distract the audience's attention from *that* statement, and so they're figuring out a rebuttal.

H: Well, how do you handle that?

E: Well, then you've got an unresponsive person, you see. The question is, can you teach him to listen? Can you teach him to postpone till next month any rebuttal, if there is a rebuttal necessary? Can you teach him this isn't a debate, with rebuttal and counter-rebuttals?

H: I know, I have a pair like that at the moment.

W: Yes, I've seen several.

H: That's an example of how you tell how responsive they are when they're in the room, but when you're trying to decide whether to bring the mate in or not?

E: If my patient wants the mate brought in, and if I think the mate should be brought in, I try to figure out, from what scanty or generous amount of information my patient gives me, the type of personality. Soon as

I have formulated an idea of the mate, then I start formulating it the other way. The humorous way, and not the unkind and hostile way.

W: You say when your patient wants the spouse brought in – are there situations when the patient either doesn't indicate this or is pretty dubious about it, that you still might recommend it?

E: Oh yes. I think of my patient yesterday that you missed seeing. She's coming to me secretly. She doesn't know whether or not she will want me to see her husband. I have the feeling already that I won't want to see her husband.

H: That you *won't* want to?

E: Yes. My reason for that is this: They've been married – what is it – six years? She mentioned yesterday how he throws up to her as recent as yesterday a misunderstanding they had in the first week of marriage.

H: That's a reason for not bringing him in?

E: On a minor matter. It was an incidental thing. I won't give the exact thing, but I can give you a comparison. A spilling of a glass of wine on her dress so it had to be sent to the cleaners. Six years is an awful long time to remember things as inconsequential as that. If he can remember that, how many other inconsequential things is he going to remember? His wife has worked through all of the marriage to further their home, except during the time she was pregnant. And she worked part of the time when she was pregnant.

H: Well, why does this tell you not to bring the man in?

E: How much of my time is he going to spend dragging up all of these inconsequential things? What's his interest really going to be?

W: What is your alternative then? Do you think that nothing can be done about him, or that something can be done about him, or that something can be done about the situation by leaving him off to the side?

E: Well, the thing is this: The husband's girlfriend is coming in to ask her for a divorce. The husband sees nothing wrong with the girlfriend coming in and asking his wife to give him a divorce. What chances of saving the marriage? Is there a marriage there to be saved? Yes, she thinks there is. I don't think so. I can be mistaken, but so can she. But I better consider very, very seriously the possibility of her adjustments after a divorce, after a separation. Her adjustments in a continued marriage with a husband who behaves that way.

* * *

H: When you get some idea of how responsive a husband is, this affects your decision on whether to bring the husband in or not. Now if he seems to you a responsive person, do you assume that you can just work with the wife and he'll adapt to her changes?

E: After you've worked with the wife for a while and you've inquired about her husband's reaction to her changes, you frequently get an awfully good measurement.

H: If he's reacting wrongly you'd bring him in then?

E: Sometimes, if he's reacting very, very nicely, you recognize that you can speed up his reaction. If he's reacting wrong, but in what ways is he reacting wrong? If it's a sort of jealous wrong reaction, and if he's jealous about the improvements in his wife, then you haul him in very quickly. Sometimes you exploit that jealous reaction by getting him to praise all of these changes in his wife, intensify his jealous reactions. Then only so gently mention, and indirectly mention, the possible changes in his own behavior. He shows you. What is the motivation for a child learning in school? To please himself, that's right. To please the teachers, that's right. To show his classmates, that's right. To achieve learning too. There's a multiplicity of motivations for learning in a classroom. You've got to have *some* motivation.

H: Well, when you see, say a wife, and she tells you all about the marriage, and it seems to you you'd better bring the husband in, what you sometimes get is a reluctance on the part of the wife, because of her attachment to you, to have the husband come in and give the other side of the picture. Do you run across that?

E: I correct that immediately. I know a great deal is said about this transference relationship, and while I like to have my patients like me, and like me immensely, I want them to like me in such a fashion that I, as a therapist, can be pleased. If it pleases me to see the husband, the transference to me is going to induce them to want me to see their husband, not an inhibition.

H: Well, what if the wife's been slanting things, or feels she has?

E: When she feels that, I've already provided for that. Because I always stress to the patient the importance of giving *your* side of the story. I express the importance of that.

H: That implies there's another side?

W: It also means you want to hear their side as their side, without meaning that I only want to hear your side if it's the truth, so that it can be only one part of the picture without any derogation to it.

E: Yes. And I tell the patient, "In fact, in telling your side of the story, I'm perfectly willing for you to exaggerate it wrongly." I should be. But what does that do? It emphasizes the fact that there is another side of the story. It emphasizes the fact that perhaps they exaggerate wrongly, but they share that same defect with their mate in exaggerating wrongly.

W: Well, we have another question that I think is probably closely related to this one: Suppose the wife has come in and told you a lot of information she considers very secret and confidential. Then the husband comes into the picture. How do you handle what she has told you privately up until then?

E: I tell my patients, "Ordinarily everything you say to me will be confidential. Now if there's something that you tell me that is highly confidential, and I need to discuss it with your husband, I am going to lead the conversation around in such a fashion that he tells me the same thing. Now you know that your husband is stepping out on you. He doesn't know that you know it. He would be utterly furious, and he would leave you, if he were aware that you knew it. He's scared to death that you will know it, and yet you do know it. Since you're my patient he's going to avoid telling me that for fear I'll betray it. Nevertheless, I've got to lead the conversation around in such a fashion that he will 'spontaneously' tell me that. But I'm not going to tell you whether or not he's told me."

H: Well, that's a complicated one.

W: A nice little twist in that.

E: Don't you see what that does? It makes her realize I will keep things confidential, but I'll keep things confidential for her husband. I'm going to do the same thing with her husband, you know. So they are going to have an absolute implicit trust in me, because I've told each of them, "I won't tell you what your mate has discussed with me." There's a need for discussion. There's an evergrowing need, and I'm going to utilize that need. The first thing they know, she's telling him that she knows, and he's telling her what she already knows, and then they can come down to brass tacks and work out their adjustments, which they can't possibly do as long as she keeps her secret and he keeps his secrets.

W: Well, somehow you tell them you'll keep things confidential in such a way that it puts pressure on them to talk more to each other.

E: That's right.

W: But I don't quite see yet how it's done.

E: I'm doing the secret keeping, you see.

W: You're taking over the keeping of secrets so they have to take over the talking.

E: Yes.

H: And you don't advise them more directly that they should talk to each other about these things?

E: When I tell you I'll keep your secret, you feel very comfortable about it. You are at liberty to choose whom else you can disclose your secret to. Because you know I won't ever disclose it, and I'll keep it, and so you have betrayed it to me, disclosed it to me, and you've done it safely. You've learned that it's possible to disclose your secret safely. Here's a secret that requires disclosure and I'm keeping it.

H: Now this reminds me of a couple I've seen in which the wife was hospitalized for addiction to Seconal. While she was in there, her husband had a vasectomy without her knowledge or permission. About two months later, she discovered she was pregnant. He argued that possibly it was because he didn't go back for that final check-up, and therefore he was still fertile at the time. They had intercourse two or three months after the vasectomy. Now she's all indignant and says she wants her husband to agree one hundred percent that it's her child and his child. Well now, it seems pretty obvious to me that it isn't.

E: It is pretty obvious to me that there's an excellent possibility.

H: That it *is*?

E: Yes.

H: On what basis?

E: Why hasn't the husband done one particular thing?

H: Which particular thing?

E: Go back and get a sperm count.

H: Well, I know he could do that.

E: Why hasn't he?

H: I don't think he wants to find out.

E: He doesn't want to find out. You never suggest that sperm count. In fact, you don't want him to, because a sperm count can be faulty. There's a vas deferens on this side and a vas deferens on this side, is that correct? But let's go into anatomy. Sometimes you have an accessory vas deferens too. You've cut the one, you haven't cut the accessory. The accessory now and then allows the passage of sperm cells. Now and then you can get a positive sperm count. In medical economics there's been a recent report of vasectomized fathers with systematic repetitious sperm counts and the discovery that the men *are* fertile, but not consistently fertile. There's a lot of speculation, and it is known anatomically that you can have accessory vas deferens. It is known that sometimes in spite of knotting and tying and cutting out of a section that anatomically there is a restoration of the vas deferens. It has been found out that sometimes you have viable sperm as late as three months after the vasectomy.

H: Given this couple, what would you do with them?

E: I would tell the man, "You know what the betting is. That you aren't the father. But now let's look into all of the possibilities." I've already mentioned the *one* possibility of another man. Then I proceed to mention the possibility of an accessory vas deferens, the possibility of a restoration of the vas deferens, the possibility of the continued viability of the sperm cells. Then I mention the same thing is true on the right side as is on the left side, so that's three more possibilities. (Laughter) That's right. When I do exactly the same thing for the woman, she thinks, well isn't that beautiful, I've got this defense, and this defense, and this defense, and this, and this and this. It's nice to have so many defenses, how about this one? If she's guilty, she'll tell me. You see? So she gets defenses for her secret. If she's innocent, you will see that very, very lovely look of relief from a false accusation. If she is guilty, then you will see, "Now I have one more defense. I can share my guilty secret, and I've got all of those defenses."

H: Well, even if she's guilty and you provide all those defenses, you still put a pretty good idea in her mind that she might have had an affair but she could still be pregnant by her husband.

E: That's right. Then you've created another problem. How does she want to regard the baby? As her husband's and hers? Or as her lover's and hers? Sometimes when you see the woman, she is really guilty, but she can't quite muster up the courage to share that with you. You discuss abstractly that additional problem of how, in another such case, there is this problem of how the child shall be regarded. Since it can be the husband's, when she starts analyzing that problem and thinking about it, then she steps over the line and tells you the things she couldn't quite bring her courage up to. So then she has a problem of reality adjustment in the future.

H: Suppose a wife did tell you that she had an affair and this wasn't her husband's baby? What would you push for in that situation?

E: One of the things that I tell a bride-to-be who's had affairs, "Your sexual life is your own private sexual life. Nobody else can understand it. You can tell your psychiatrist; if you're Catholic you can tell your priest. But you never tell your father, your mother, your husband, and your son and your daughter. Because they're emotionally involved with you and they just can't understand. They're emotionally involved. You need to tell it to somebody who *can understand.*"

H: And who's that?

E: Your psychiatrist, and your priest if you're Catholic. There are too many marriages broken up. A very, very nice girl gets herself seduced because she knew no defenses at all to protect herself. Then she marries a chap who has seduced any number of girls and gone out with any number of chippies. He finds his wife isn't a virgin, and then he throws it at her for the rest of her life, which is wrong. She was literally a nice girl, reared never knowing anything about sex, and she found herself caught in a situation she didn't understand. She didn't know what defenses were.

H: Getting back to this now, what you seem to be implying is that you would encourage the wife not to tell the husband?

E: That's right. How's that going to improve the matter? You're going to disrupt the marriage. You're going to create a wretched situation for that child. You're endangering the marriage. You're endangering the wife's status. You're endangering the child's status, because when he gets to be a teenager and a pain in the neck, his foster father is going to call him a stinking bastard. I can think of a very happy home. Three children. Square-faced, blue-eyed, heavy-jawed. Father is very proud of his three sons that look so much like him. They were fathered by another man whom his wife picked out because of that man's resemblance to her husband, whose ancestry was similar to her husband's, German ancestry. Her husband married her under false pretenses. Never told her he had a vasectomy. She found out from one of his mistresses that he had had a vasectomy.

H: He assumes now that it wasn't complete?

E: That's right. He was my patient. He was a college man. He's never gone back for a sperm count. He is never going to go back.

W: Not now.

E: I didn't forbid him to. I laid out everything for him and for his wife. I'll admit that I loaded my frank and complete and honest discussion (laughter) by inflections and intonations. He's exceedingly proud of his three sons. His wife over the years hasn't deluded herself, but she literally reacts as if they were his sons.

H: Where did she get the idea to have them this way?

E: She came in and told me what she was going to do. All she wanted was helpful suggestions so that her plans would be foolproof. It is a happy marriage, and the man is socially and economically successful. He's got a lovely home. He's got a big business. He's a well-known businessman.

H: So you are willing to keep a secret of one partner from another partner?

E: Why certainly. I haven't got the right to go and blab to Joe that Jean's children aren't his. That'll rob him of every bit of happiness, and he's happy in his marriage. It will rob him of his children, he's happy with his children. He's got a great deal of pride in those blue eyes, that heavy chin that his three sons have, that square face that they have.

W: Well, you know if you told him that they are not his children, that wouldn't really be the truth either.

E: Emotionally they are his children. Genetically no.

W: Genetically no. But the more I've seen of raising children, it's raising the children to a very great extent that makes them your children.

E: Yes. And that wife's very, very careful search for a man of her husband's stature, general build, German ancestry, general appearance, college graduate—that utterly cold-blooded, calculating search. That woman wanted children. She married – what did I call him, Jack or Jim or Joe – with a promise that she could have at least two children. He promised them. He felt very guilty when he told me all about it.

H: Peculiar marriage.

E: What about these cultures where a man isn't going to marry a girl unless she's demonstrated her capacity to bear children? What father? The father that came to her in a bachelor's house.

H: What I mean by a peculiar marriage is that it's a marriage based on deceit to start with. The man doesn't tell his wife the truth. She counters by having three children and doesn't tell him the truth, even though *she's* aware of it. So you have a marriage starting, I think, with considerable distance between the two and continuing that way.

E: All right, now take this example. You have two small children and one hits the other. You know what can go on, a battle royal for the rest of the day. So you step out and you say to Nellie, "Johnny hit you and it hurt. Johnny, is that right?" "Yes, I hit her." "Well, do you want to fight for the rest of the day or shall we let Nellie hit you in the way you hit her, and then you're equal?" So you cancel the one wrong with another wrong, but it's done openly with the children. Now Joe deceived Anne with his vasectomy and his promises that she could have at least two children. Then Anne discovered through a set of circumstances that he had had a vasectomy. She's never let him know that she knows that, so he's got his secret about the vasectomy. But so does she have her secret about the vasectomy.

W: You're suggesting, maybe, sometimes two wrongs *do* make a right?

E: Two wrongs *do* make a right. So they both share a guilty secret about that vasectomy. He doesn't know that she knows it. She's keeping it a secret too. He promised her at least two children, guiltily. She's had at least two children, guiltily. They share a common secret. Now you will say there's a lot of sophistry in that, but how do we react? Do we fall in love with a girl because of this logical reason, or that logical reason? My father and mother have been married happily for 68 years. My father says the most charming thing about my mother is that her nose points west – in other words, she's got a crooked nose. Can you imagine a more illogical reason? (Laughter) But how do we behave emotionally? On pure reason and logic? So you deal with patients in accord with normal, illogical behavior, illogical emotional reasons. I know a man who said the thing that attracted him to his wife, first time he saw her, was rather a puzzle – she had a little bubble of spit in the corner of her mouth. (Laughter) That's right. They've been happily married, to my knowledge, for at least 20 years. The next time he saw her she still had that little bit of, little spit in the corner, well that's an intriguing girl, how does she do it? (Laughter)

H: When you get a couple dealing with each other in a certain sort of a way – now when you get an individual and he's dealing with you in a certain sort of a way, you accept that and utilize it – if you get a couple dealing with each other in a certain sort of a way, do you tend to accept that and exaggerate it or utilize that too?

E: This concept of geometrical progression that I pointed out to you. I so often use that and sometimes I ask the person to manipulate his wife one millionth of one percent less. (Laughter) Now you can't possibly refuse to do that. Then there's two millionths of one percent. You've asked him to quit dealing with his wife in a certain way – you do the same thing with the wife.

Sometimes you aid them in handling the other their way and let them turn it over to you.

H: You mean they're handling the mate in a certain way, and you manage to aid them in doing that. Then they can leave it up to you to do it rather than them doing it. You can now direct it?

E: The husband and wife who came to me because they always battled when they went to the movies. It always worked out this way: The husband would ask his wife, "How about going to the movies this week?" She'd say, "Fine, if we don't quarrel." He would always tell her, "Well, you pick out the night, and you pick out the movie and we'll go." She'd say, "Of course I'll pick out the night and the movie and somehow or other we'll wind up at a different movie on a different night." He would always promise, but he'd always make that business engagement, or he'd forget something that was imperative, that she had to admit was imperative, and they always went to a different movie.

So what did I do? I suggested to them that they pick out a certain night and a certain movie and let me know. Then I told the wife to choose the movie. It was the last night that movie would be shown. I arranged that as soon as I had my calendar straight, I'd give them an evening appointment. So the wife picked out a movie, and I knew which one it was. It was the last night. I notified the husband about the evening appointment. I had an opening. They showed up. She was mad. Her husband suddenly realized, and he told me what a stinking trick it was. I agreed with him. I showed him my calendar. It was the only evening I had. They had wanted an evening appointment, if possible, and yet he felt it was a stinking trick. What was he telling me? His own maneuvering was a stinking trick. When the wife saw him telling me that I had worked a stinking trick, that smug smile on her face, which encouraged her husband to denounce me even more. Then she told him, "You know, you're telling the doctor it's a stinking trick, when it's the same trick you pull on me all the time." He said, "Well, that's right; the doctor couldn't help it, and I couldn't help it." Then he said, "You know, could you have given us an appointment next week?" I said, "Yes. That's right. I could have but I didn't think of it." (Laughter)

W: You were too busy thinking of giving them an appointment that night.

E: And he said, "But you could have thought about it, and I could think about it too." Another demonstration.

* * *

A couple came in here rowing fearfully on this question of buying a house. The husband said, "We're going to buy a house, and your mother is not going to live with us." She said, "We're going to buy a house, and mother *is* going to live with us." They both gave me a very nice history of mother. Mother was living with them in that sprawling, poor-grade house in South Phoenix. There was quite a patch of land there and they had enough water. Mother is a nice, old, neatly-groomed woman. Son-in-law is a college graduate, daughter is a college graduate; they both teach. The mother was a grade school graduate, a rather intelligent woman. But she lives with her son and daughter. Daughter is sterile, no children. They had a horrible battle. After they decribed mother to me, I drew my own conclusions about mother. Mother had very fixed hours. She always went to bed at a certain time. She always got up at a certain time. I've forgotten what items of food mother always had for breakfast. They had no such rigidity about their breakfast. Mother visited her friends in that neighborhood with a certain regularity. She never visited certain friends on a Sunday; other friends she did. Some friends she visited in the afternoon, never in the evening. Others she visited in the evening only. Mother did quite a bit of reading. She had educational books for certain days of the week, novels for certain other days, and weekends she always read the Bible. On Sunday mornings, and Sunday afternoons, at a certain hour she picked up her Bible and read. Nothing altered that.

I encouraged them to go and buy a house. They searched all over Phoenix, and mother had talked to them about moving with them, and the difficulties of packing up. I told the husband, "Your wife says that mother goes with you. You say she doesn't. Get the house purchased. That's a big enough problem, because even though there's no segregation here, you'll find that real estate agents are going to be showing you certain houses, that the price goes up horribly." They were persistent. They finally bought a house with a nice extra room and a den that could be made into a parlor for mother.

They told mother, in accordance with my instructions, that they were moving and what assistance did she want in packing? The mother looked at them in absolute horror. That woman was fixed and rigid and regular and patterned in her behavior. When the opportunity came to move, mother said, "I'm not moving away from here." Daughter tried to plead with mother, but mother for the first time suddenly realized that she wasn't going to leave her friends. She wasn't going to leave her garden. She wasn't going to leave the familiarity of that place. Then the daughter and the husband came back and said, "You know you told us to postpone the quarrel about mother living with us until after we had the house. You told me to go along with my wife. How did you know mother wouldn't move?" I knew she wouldn't. Not with that sort of a rigid pattern, always the same food for breakfast. You couldn't put that kind of a woman into a strange neighborhood, a strange house. Not when she visits her friends in this neighborhood – certain ones in the afternoon, certain ones in the evening.

H: So the young folks were having a battle about something that would never come to fruition anyhow?

E: That's right. Those two teachers are tremendously grateful. They came back later and said, "You know, we've always had minor disagreements. We're not having those anymore. We wait until the issue really comes up."

H: Postpone the quarrel?

E: Postpone the quarrel.

W: In the case of this couple and mother, did the mother give them to understand that she *would* move beforehand?

E: The mother really expected to move; daughter expected, husband expected mother to move. I knew there was no possibility for mother to recognize it. She couldn't possibly grasp it because she's too tied up with her rigid patterns. Not until she was confronted, when she suddenly realized she couldn't get out of her patterns. The daughter wouldn't have any appreciation because mother is intelligent, she reads good books and good novels. She's an intelligent woman. That's right. Mother's still living in that place, and she's happy there. The husband couldn't realize it. There were no ways for them to realize it. But they could recognize that they were happily married. They only had each other, no children, and here they're venturing into a major move – a good home, in a much better neighborhood. It would be a difficult thing, and they really ought not to quarrel. Because how could they find a good home if they were at swords' points? They didn't know how it was going to work out, but they did agree that they ought to postpone the battle, and let coming events settle it. While they described all of their pleasant and good adjustments in that poor home, which was actually, of course, a good home psychologically and emotionally, they didn't realize what they were telling me about mother. They were too close to mother to have any understanding of that rigid pattern formation.

* * *

H: Well, now with some couples when you see them interacting in a certain way, the husband doing certain things with the wife, you're likely to do the same thing with the wife as a demonstration for both of them.

E: Yes.

H: In what other ways do you accept what they're already doing? I mean, they're dealing with each other in a way that's obviously reinforcing. He does something, she does something which forces him to do what he just did, which forces her to do what she just did, and they go back and forth on it.

E: I can think of another couple. She resented the way he took her out to dinner. He always insisted on at least a $25 bill for the two of them. Then he'd give a $5 to $10 tip. So she went out with him, first securing permission to order whatever she pleased, and she and I worked it out. I told her husband to let her have her own way on this particular outing in the restaurant. She ordered filet mignon – $5.75 I think it was. Then after eating part, she said, "You know, this really is good, I wish I had ordered this other," and she ordered another $5 meat dish. She ordered a third. She ran the bill up thoroughly. She gave the waiter a $15 tip. She paid for the meal, and she gave the waiter a $15 tip. He looked at all that wasted food and that great big tip, because she didn't finish the third thing, because that wasn't so good, and she was tired of the restaurant. He came and told me about it, and he said, "You know, it's just as stupid as my own behavior; did you put my wife up to it?" I said, "Did you see your behavior in any better way? Don't you hope I put her up to it?" (Laughter) Yes, he hoped I had. You see, that took the accusation out of it – out of the denunciatory thing.

H: And made it an example?

E: And forcing them to another emotional attitude by saying, "Don't you hope I did?"

H: Now that's an example of getting the wife to do what the husband is doing.

E: Yes. He's going to keep on wasting his money that way until he sees it done.

W: I'm curious how you arranged one detail within that. How did you arrange that she would be buying the dinner?

E: I told her to take it out of her own special, personal allowance and to tell her husband, "You've always taken me out to dinner. You've always bought me wonderful dinners. Now even though it's not customary, I'd like to do it."

W: Just this once.

E: Just this once. (Laughter)

H: What we keep pushing up against here, I think, is this question of how husband and wife reinforce each other's behavior. Now I've been seeing a series of anxious wives who can't leave the house. In just about every case, when the wife does start to leave the house, the husband starts to get upset. You can see it at the session. I raised the question with the wife about leaving, and she said, "Well, maybe I'll drive to San Francisco," which is 30 miles. The husband said, "Well, there's no need to go that far." There's no reason why his wife couldn't go to San Francisco. But each move to go, he puts a damper on.

E: That's right.

H: Well, how do you handle that?

E: He can't stand to have her go, can he?

H: Right.

E: Then you tell the husband, "Is it all right for you to go with her and drive the car?"

H: Well, in this particular case she can go if somebody goes with her. The issue is around her going alone. If she has a chaperone, it's all right.

E: Yes. Well, he's got long, long practice in this matter of his wife going here and there. Now what are the words I used? He's had long practice and anxiety about his wife going here and going there. Is that right?

H: Yes.

E: What is the essential word in that statement? From what does his anxiety derive? What is the word I used? His wife *going* here and there, isn't that right?" *Going* is the essential word, isn't it? Now what happens when his wife *comes* from Mesa to Phoenix? Never mind how she got there. When she's coming alone from Mesa to Phoenix. You take the word "going" and you transfer it to "coming" back home. She's not going away from home, she's coming home.

H: All right. I can see how you might do this, but I don't see how you do it.

W: You mean, in your case you would get around to talking about her *coming*, how he might feel about her *coming*, from San Francisco back home.

E: Oh, I commit him to the fact that he could not tolerate his wife going from Phoenix to Mesa. And I don't know how many times I'd use that word "going" unobtrusively. But I really commit him to it. I would have "going" here, and "going" there, and "going," "going," "going," "going." I'd commit him, I'd tie him to it, I'd condition him to that. Then I would discuss something about a trip that he and his wife made. I'd find out about something of that sort. And the particular driving on the way home, they were "coming" home, and use that word "coming" and "coming" and "coming" and "coming," always in a completely pleasurable fashion. You know, I've built up the situation how comfortable he feels, there's always somebody with his wife when she's going. Then I'd have her come home alone. Have her follow the same route that he and she had followed coming home. But what he's done is put his wife in a car, and later I can mention how his wife, "Let's see, she was going to Mesa to Phoenix on that particular day." She was, you know, *going* from Mesa to Phoenix. She was *coming* from Mesa to Phoenix, but she was going from Mesa to Phoenix.

H: So you'd get an impression that this was a need of this man, not to let her go, and transform this by shifting the "going" to "coming"?

E: Yes. You first commit him to the word "going."

CHAPTER 4

Encouraging Relapses and Giving Directives

1959. Present were Milton H. Erickson, Jay Haley, and John Weakland.

H: Another thing about couples: You get a couple who have a certain sort of a pattern which they're busy reinforcing, and you get them to do something differently, one or both of them. How do you keep them from going back to the previous pattern? How do you peg their change?

E: Oh, but you tell them that they really ought to go back to the previous pattern.

H: To try it out.

E: And select out of it that which needs to be salvaged. (Laughter) What are you doing? You're teaching them, "Don't be ashamed of that horrible past pattern, there's at least something worth salvaging." Just consider the small child with a favorite toy that he's got to discard, that he won't discard, which is all worn out. What do you do with him to get him to discard it? You salvage a part. And then he can discard it.

W: You mean, just keep the ear of that rabbit; then we can get rid of all the tatters with the rest of it.

E: That's right. When your couple goes back to that pattern, they really ought to go back to salvage some one little thing, because then *they* are earmarking it for complete disposal. They've had plenty of lifelong experience of doing that sort of thing. We all have.

H: Well, related to this now, when you get a couple who've spent some years managing to keep some distance between themselves by antagonizing each other, when they start to get close, and you manage to produce change so that they do get closer, how do you keep them from panicking about this?

E: How do I keep them from what?

H: From getting in a panic about this. Because naturally they're going to get a little threatened if they get closer or they would have got closer sooner.

E: The panic reaction is when they discover they've got a brand-new pattern of life that they're beginning to develop.

H: They're beginning to enjoy each other.

E: Yes. I tell them, "How do you really handle a brand-new set of dishes? Because you're worried about breaking some."

W: Handle with care.

E: Handle with care (laughs) because it's valuable. They're tremulous about handling that brand-new set of dishes, and they've had plenty of experience. Take your own reaction when you get a new pair of eyeglasses. You never put them down like that (tossing them down).

W: The set of dishes might even be something where they could conceive of handling them carefully together, and each one sort of cautioning the other one even, which is what they're doing with a thing like dishes.

E: Yes. I would likely use something as an illustration where there can be a loss without a destruction. Sure, you can lose a cup, you can lose a saucer, you can lose a part of a plate, yet you've still got your dishes.

H: On this, there is one of the things that is unclear to me when you handle a couple, and it's one of the things we keep running into with various schools of handling families. That is the question of how much of what you see the couple are doing with each other do you make explicit to them that they're doing to each other? Apparently you do very little of this.

E: Very, very little. You see, most therapy is directed to the idea of presenting therapeutic solutions instead of presenting to the patients their ways of living happily in the world of reality. That is, you explain to children – good sibling relationships are established by an attitude of sharing. Now the reality situation isn't that. Sometimes you want to give your brother an apple. Sometimes you want your brother to give *you* an apple. That's not saying exactly the same thing. In the one way you phrase it, you present it in terms of therapeutic concepts. Sibling relationships. Sometimes you want your brother to give you an apple, and sometimes you want to give your brother an apple. You've described sibling relationships. But too often it's done in therapeutic terminology. When the patient has to live in a reality situation wherein he sits in *his* chair and he eats *his* apple, and so on.

H: Well, I'm not thinking so much of when the therapist gives them a therapeutic solution. One of the theories of therapies with couples or families is that you bring them together and you get them to express their feelings about each other; then you point out to them how they're dealing with each other. Now I gather that you don't do anything of this sort. That when you see how they're dealing with each other you don't discuss with *them* how they're dealing with each other.

E: I try to avoid that. See how you hurt sister's feelings? See how you hurt brother's feelings? See how you cheated brother? See how you cheated sister?

H: Well, it isn't done quite that way. (Laughs)

E: No, I know, but I'm rewording it.

W: I suppose you can carry that to what you would do instead at the same level of terms, instead of, "See how you treated sister."

E: Yes. "See how you could have given sister something instead of cheating her." So you've accused him of a double sin; he cheated her, and he didn't even give her anything.

W: But he could have?

E: But he could have.

W: So you can.

E: Yes, but he's committed two sins: He's cheated her and he didn't give her.

W: But you're holding out the possibility of redemption here.

E: Yes.

* * *

E: I am seeing a very handsome couple. The husband is an only child of extremely intelligent parents. He is a capable college graduate. The girl is an only daughter of very nice parents, except that her father had some combination of diseases – arthritis plus emphysema. He had a tremendous amount of pain, and he was bedridden much of her childhood. Her father was the kind of man who could sit quietly with somebody and commune. He concealed his pain. He was cheerful, enthusiastic, interested in his daughter. He taught her the actual value of money: "Be willing to spend money, but purchase the values money represents. When you fall in love, fall in love on a permanent basis and really, thoroughly, enjoy being in love. Have a home that's a happy home, give your all, nothing's too small to do to contribute to the happiness of the home. Fatigue is part of life, pain is part of life, disappointment is part of life. But happiness is the major part." The type of thoughtful philosophy that such a father would give his daughter. The girl had received no sex instruction before she married. The young man had been very thoroughly indulged by his parents. He had sex experience.

Three months after the marriage, the girl discovered addresses and telephone numbers lying around the house. A flushed face and a patent lie was the explanation for those telephone numbers. He even told her to call them if she didn't believe him, but his face told her she ought not to call. But it wasn't a garage, and she finally did call.

When she got pregnant with the first son, it was all her fault, her husband said. She pointed out that she had worn a diaphragm in accordance with his request, that he refused to wear a condom, and that he had told her that she didn't need to bother to put the contraceptive jelly in the diaphragm. "What the hell was she so slow about?" He didn't even let her check, as she always did when she inserted the diaphragm, after it was in place, to see that it was really in place. Then, after that night, he said, "Well, you won't get pregnant from once or twice more," and so the next night, and the next night, he insisted on having intercourse without any contraception. He still said it was all her fault. If he didn't exercise common sense, she should have.

When she was three months pregnant, various women began to call for – let's call him Bobby – with cooing voices. He said he didn't know any of these women at all. The cooing voices left their telephone numbers. He left slips of paper around the house with similar telephone numbers on them. She gave birth to her son. Her husband was out all night that night. He was out the night she returned from the hospital.

He bought her a $30,000 house; he turned over all

of his checks to her. She was to pay all the bills. Of course, it was her fault if his check didn't cover the amount of bills. He incurred the bills, she paid them. It was her fault if she overdrew the checking account. It was her fault if there was not enough money in the bank.

You know, there isn't anything to do with that guy. She separated from him temporarily, and he took the swankiest apartment possible in a nice hotel. Her final reaction after seven years of that sort of thing is to develop absolute frigidity. Her husband is out of work. She makes about as much sexual response to him as she would make to that piece of driftwood. He has gone for six months being an absolutely, completely courteous chap in every regard, considerate in every way. He held down his expenditures, except that there's this one thing; he just can't see that what he needs to do is get rid of that expensive house, that great big yard, the yard man that costs so much a week.

He took his family and son out to the races. He said, "I'm not interested in going to the races, but we've got nothing to do this afternoon." His wife said, "I'm not interested in going to the races, and sonny's too young. I'd rather go to a show or something like that." He said, "Well, we've never really gone to the races, we might as well go." The wife said, "Well, I'm not going to enjoy it, it's boring, I'm just not interested in even seeing the races on television." He said, "Neither am I, but we've never been, let's go." They went out. He hauled out of the trunk three of those folding chairs. She looked at them and said, "How much do they cost?" "Oh, I got them at a bargain sale at $4 apiece." "Well, what did you buy them for?" "To go to the races." He sat down for about 20 minutes, and the thing was boring, so he said, "Let's go home."

She said, "Well, we could at least use those chairs for a whole race and get that much value out of them." He said, "I'll give the chairs away." She said, "We can't afford that money. Is there any way of returning the chairs and getting at least part of the money back?" He said, "No, I bought them on a sale; there's no return." "What are you going to do with the chairs?" "Let's just throw them away." She said, "We can't afford that sort of thing." He said that in an utterly objective, dispassionate way, "Throw them away." I discussed that with him. He said, "Well, it's only $12. I made more than that in poker the other night. I won $250."

I asked the wife, "What do you want to do?" She said, "Well, I'm completely unhappy. I'll sit home. I'll watch my son grow up. I don't like this. I cringe at the thought of his getting in bed; he might accidentally touch me." I said, "What do you think about your body? You're a beautiful woman, you've got a very attractive body." She said, "Yes, I could have an affair with somebody; a lot of his friends have propositioned me. I can't have an affair with them; they're friends of *his*. I do know that the idea of an affair is very, very tempting, but I'm not going to have an affair at least in my present frame of mind."

Now I've seen them – I've seen each of them at least six times. I'm no further along than I was at the beginning. I can't budge that girl. She's twice told me, "I could be tempted to have an affair." There's no mistaking what she means. "I could be tempted." Her husband is again laying – accidentally – telephone numbers around. When I tell him that he's doing it, he says, "No, you must be mistaken. I know I did that several years ago, but I've corrected it." I would say to him, "But you are still doing it." He said, "No, you're completely mistaken, I'm not." I can say to him, "Well, suppose I gave you a telephone number, do you recognize it?" He said, "Yes, but I don't know how you ever figured out that I would recognize that telephone number." Now if I can give him a telephone number that he recognizes, and he can't figure out how I got it, I've asked him, "If I showed you that telephone number in your handwriting, now what would you say?" "Well, that's impossible, and yet if you did I'd have to reach the conclusion that my wife forged it." "Then the question arises, how would your wife know what telephone number to forge?" He said, "I just can't understand it at all."

H: You know, I'm not very clear on what you think is the problem with this couple.

E: I don't know what the problem is. This woman is perfectly willing – well, she isn't entering into the therapeutic situation. She tells me that she could be tempted to have an affair. She's got that history of a father that she adored.

H: Who was undoubtedly a disappointment to her.

E: Mmmmm, and here I am old enough to be her father, and she could be tempted sexually to have an affair. That much I know about her. So passive, so polite, and so courteous. But I'm getting nowhere. The husband – how can he be that blindly stupid?

H: It's a real art.

E: It's a real art he's accomplished.

H: You know, one of the points of view that we have, that I haven't heard you talk about particularly, is a kind of Sullivanian approach that a couple doesn't get too close without getting in a bit of a panic. That they manipulate each other so that they don't get to each other. If a wife is concerned about her husband getting too close to her, sexually or otherwise, she's likely to provoke him in such a way that she can have a justifiable excuse for withdrawing. The husband is likely to do the same with the wife.

E: Yes, and therefore, with that type of patient, you know that she's going to provoke her husband so that she will have a legitimate excuse to withdraw. You know that he is going to arouse her, to attract her, and at the same time he'll do something so that she will do something so he has a legitimate reason for withdrawing. It's a beautiful bit of manipulation.

H: Now when they're threatened with getting close together, he's going to leave some notes with telephone numbers around.

E: When that type of patient comes in to me, I like to help the woman devise the measure that forces her husband to withdraw. I like to help the husband devise the measure that forces the wife to withdraw.

H: This is again accepting and encouraging what they're already doing.

E: Yes. As soon as I do the devising, they become dependent upon me for devising. Then I can change the maneuver.

W: And somehow it doesn't seem possible to take over what they are doing in this case that you've been telling us about?

E: I don't know of a single, solitary thing that I can do.

H: You wouldn't instruct the husband in this case to leave a phone number around?

E: He would blindly disregard me and continue to leave them around. (Laughter) It would be as if I hadn't even told him.

H: He must be quite a character.

W: There's no way you could tell him to leave 50 phone numbers around every week?

E: Another thing that he does every time he overspends and his wife rebels so horribly: He calls up his father and asks for $1,000. And gets it. Of course, that's spent on debts. But he and she are paying the mortgage on the house. That comes out of his paycheck. But his wife regards that as a falsification. She doesn't feel that just because the money that goes to the mortgage comes out of his paycheck that they're really paying.

W: She feels they're not really paying it off because he's getting the thousand dollars from papa to pay on other things he's getting into.

E: Yes. She thinks the $12 for the chairs should have gone on the mortgage and not be something that father-in-law pays off along with lots of other stupid debts.

W: Well, this brings us to a question – the most specific question we've had. In this case Milton doesn't think he can instruct this man apparently to do something, and we were going to raise the question, what do you do with people who won't do what you tell them?

H: Yes.

W: We find that some people will do what you say, and other people seem very hard to give a suggestion to, to carry out something.

E: The woman, I'm pretty certain, would very, very gladly have an affair with me or would take my advice to have an affair with someone else. But that would be the complete destruction of any therapeutic relationship, whether she had an affair with me or with someone else. The man just isn't doing anything.

W: With him you feel that you practically can't tell him anything, and with her you would only tell her what would be the wrong thing to do.

E: Yes.

H: You couldn't tell her to reject her husband?

E: No.

H: What brings them in to you?

E: What brings them in? Periodically the husband loses his temper in a small boy fashion and smashes the panel in the door, picks up an ashtray and fires it through the window. Picks up a chair and crashes it on the floor and wrecks it. Then he tells her, "But you won't have sexual relations with me."

H: So that's how she came in? Did you suggest they both come in?

E: No. A friend of theirs who attended one of my seminars knew them personally, visited their home. They were very, very fond of him. They are intelligent people, they are likeable people, they're charming. That seminarian, that physician, became aware of that situation, and when he found out they were moving out to Arizona, he said, "Do you want to see Dr. Erickson?" That's how they came to me. The wife said, "It's a wretched home situation; there's no lovemaking. I can't stand to have him touch me. I can't stand that little-boy outburst of temper. He blames me; maybe that's right. But we can be sitting looking at television and all of a sudden he gets up and fires an ashtray through a window. We can't afford that. I didn't see anything on the television that made him do that. I know darn well there's something on the television that he saw that precipitated it." She thinks he needs therapy for his tendency to be a Don Juan. She thinks it's psychologically and somatically wrong for her as a young woman to live a life of abstinence.

H: Well, you often would talk about a couple like this, or a case like this, and point out something you did that resolves something. What is it that makes it so difficult with these two?

E: Her utter objective passivity, her intellectualization. It's hard for her, a young woman, healthy, to be sexually abstinent.

H: How come they haven't separated, haven't divorced?

E: They did separate temporarily, and he rented the expensive suite in the hotel. They have this son. The son is very much devoted to both parents.

W: Well now, renting the suite, she has to keep charge of that?

E: Sure, she pays the bills.

W: Why?

E: He turned his paycheck over to her. Put it in the bank. She wrote the checks. Her name is on the checking account. The bills were sent to the house. She believes in being honest with tradesmen.

W: She's so proper it hurts.

E: She pays the bills. She didn't like the idea of paying for an expensive suite.

W: And she didn't like the idea of going to the races, but she went, and she didn't like the chairs.

E: She didn't continue paying for the expensive suite, because she let him come home. That way he couldn't entertain any women in that expensive suite. That's right, you know.

H: She won't get with him, and she won't get away from him?

E: Mmmm hmmm. And she won't do anything about it. She's got the situation evaluated. He is dead certain that that bland denial of his should be absolutely convincing. Have you ever seen a small child tell you a patent lie and actually expect you to believe that he didn't eat that chocolate, and you're looking at his hands and you're looking at his mouth? He didn't even know there was chocolate in the house.

W: Now I find myself wondering if she's really got that situation evaluated thoroughly enough. I mean she's thought about it, but are you sure she's really thought it through?

E: Oh yes. "You did have some orgasms when you were first married, and you enjoyed them. What type of orgasms do you think his mistresses have?" Now there's something you either explore or you purposely avoid. You see? You don't want to think about it, or you've got a tremendous morbid curiosity about it. The answer? "Well, it seems to me that different women would have different types of orgasms." That completely, highly intellectual statement, all emotional values dropped out. Can she tell you a nice joke and laugh with the greatest of amusement? Yes.

W: What I'm suggesting is: Is it not possible to get the idea across to her that she's being too emotional in all this and that she should think things over more logically?

E: I ask her can she feel her emotions thoroughly? Does she really feel happy that she can break down and use up a dozen sheets of Kleenex and then dry her tears and say, "You know, I suppose that cry did me a lot of good."

W: I have the feeling that this intellectual kick here is one limb that you don't think you can go out further on until that changes too. I get the impression you feel she's so far out on that, it is hopeless unless she comes back, and you don't feel it's possible to go and take that further the way you would take other things further.

E: I can get her to laugh, to joke, to shed genuine tears, but all of a sudden that rigid control drops in.

W: But I'm suggesting the other.

E: What?

W: That you emphasize the control.

E: I've done that.

W: What happened then?

E: Nothing. It's still her control, because she's got the same kind of deaf ear that her husband has.

W: Suppose she were a hypnotic subject, what would you do with her?

E: You see, she has a history of about three times getting very, very pleasantly drunk and raping her husband thoroughly, to his satisfaction and hers. She's told me, "So I got pleasantly high again and I thoroughly enjoyed it and I did it again, and I know I can let down my inhibitions. I know that when I'm pleasantly high I can respond to him, but I don't believe in mixing sex and alcohol. That isn't the right thing to do." She's right, you know. If she were a good hypnotic subject I'd give her a very nice dream, a dream that she was drunk. I'd see to it within that dream that she had a very nice dream and a tremendous comfort that she didn't do anything.

H: Comfort that she didn't do anything?

E: That she didn't do anything – that it was really a dream. I'd let her have the regret that she didn't take advantage of the dream. I can't put either one of them in a trance. It's that passive resistance; I can't outwit them. I'm continuing the therapy. I've told her very, very openly, "I'm getting absolutely no place with you therapeutically. Do you want to continue? If you continue, eventually I'll find your weak spot." She said, "That's the only reason for continuing, you know." Not any alarm or distress about that possibility – finding her weak spot. Her statement is, "Further, if my husband wastes money on nonsense, why shouldn't I waste it where someone is trying his level best to do something?"

W: Suppose in that context you assured her that you were doing great, but actually you just horsed around with it. This wouldn't draw fire from them either?

E: She isn't going to believe that. I can't falsify the situation. That would be unethical.

W: Oh, and she knows you wouldn't be unethical?

E: That's right.

W: You mean you couldn't push it to such a degree that she would have to recognize it?

E: You see, that deliberate statement that she could be tempted, to see if I would be unethical. Just a notification to me. Yes, she would wash all possibility of therapy right down the drain.

H: On getting patients to do what you ask, partly you do it by telling them to do what they are doing anyhow, so they're willing to do that because they're doing it anyhow. Then sometimes you catch them in a phase where they have to do it whichever way. That is, you put the time *when* to do it rather than *whether* to do it, so that they're arguing about *when* not *whether*.

E: Yes. One of my patients is on friendly terms with Mrs. Erickson. I've forgotten what the assignment was, but my patient mentioned to Mrs. Erickson what I had ordered her to do. Betty said, "Are you going to do that?" The patient said, "Why certainly, Dr. Erickson told me I had to." She said, "But why would you do anything as silly, as absurd and ridiculous as that?" She said, "Dr. Erickson told me to. I do it. I always do everything that he says, no matter what on earth it is." Betty said, "But why?" She said, "You're helpless, you do it."

W: That's what I'd like. (Laughter)

E: "You're helpless, you do it." I came out of the office and my patient said, "You know, Mrs. Erickson has been asking me why I'm going to do what you said, and I told her it was because you asked me to." I said, "That's right, I asked you to." She said, "Yes, and I'm going to do it, too." Then she turned and said, "You see how it is? He says, 'I asked you to.'"

W: And you expect them to.

E: That tremendous attitude of expectancy. How do you resist it?

W: Well, that's part of it, Jay – Milton expects they will.

H: Yes, and when they don't do it, as I recall, you once said that you made it clear they had made an error and they would never have that opportunity again. So that there'd be regret on not doing it; then they'd be more likely to do something the next time.

E: I should disguise this example very carefully. This woman, the wife of a physician, needed, let us say, a very painful medical procedure done which her husband could do very, very nicely, and quite properly, quite ethically. She was an excellent hypnotic subject who could produce any amount of anesthesia that she wanted or that she needed. Her husband was well-trained and well-experienced in hypnosis. The woman needed this procedure carried out, but didn't need it as an emergency. Her husband could produce a beautiful trance in his wife, absolutely beautiful anesthesia, up to the moment that he would start the preparation for this painful procedure. Then either the trance would disappear, or the anesthesia would disappear. He didn't want that pain there. He didn't want a general anesthetic; she didn't want a general anesthetic, it had to be done. If not today, at least tomorrow or the next day, or the next week, or some time this month. He called in several other physicians in Phoenix. Now they thought that it would be nice to do it under hypnotic anesthesia. They produced a beautiful anesthesia up to the moment. That was a horrible stalemate.

He sent her to me, and I checked into the woman's history. I told her, "Well, I don't understand why you refuse to cooperate. Why you have so little control over that. Let me find out something about your childhood. Were you a virgin when you were married, and why?" "Because I was very, very thoroughly taught to be a virgin." I said, "Weren't you ever tempted?" She said, "No. I didn't allow myself to be tempted." I said, "How modest are you," and she said, "I'm quite modest." I said, "I noticed that you were very careful to smooth your dress down. How do you sleep at night – in the raw? Or with a nightie, an abbreviated nightie? A long nightie, pajamas?" She said, "When I'm walking around I have pajamas on; in bed I can wear my pajama tops. But I don't see why you should discuss this." I said, "I've got some ideas. Do you think that you're rather modest?" She said, "Well, I buy my dresses very carefully. I don't like extreme styles. I don't like blouses cut too low. I don't like formal evening dresses that are too low, that are very extreme. I don't like these short dresses. I think a woman should be very, very careful about exposing her body." I said, "We're here alone in the office. How would you feel if I touched you on the knee?" "If you had some legitimate reason it would be all right." (Laughter) I said, "Suppose I had a legitimate reason." She said, "All right, you can go ahead and touch me on the knee." So I reached over and touched her on the knee. This way. She said, "I don't know what your legitimate reason is, there doesn't seem much sense in it." I said, "But there is a legitimate reason. I touched your knee for a legitimate reason, and I'm going to do it again also for a legitimate reason." She said, "I'll take your word for it." I said, "This time you'll find it even harder to understand. I'm going to touch your knee underneath your dress." She said, "Touching it outside my dress I can see, putting your hand under my dress I just can't see. But if you say it's a legitimate reason I'll take your word for it." So I touched her on her bare knee. I said, "Do you feel it?" She said, "Yes, and I don't like it." I said, "You're a good hypnotic subject. Why do you feel it?" She said, "I don't." I said, "That's right, you can develop an hypnotic anesthesia instantly, easily, readily." She said, "You did have a legitimate reason then, and I know it now, for touching me on the knee underneath my skirt." She said, "You know, that's astonishing. I've got that anesthesia in both legs. That anesthesia extends clear up to my hips. I simply can't move my body. That anesthesia is way up to my waistline, and I just can't get out of this chair. That isn't a pathological reaction, is it?" I said, "Now you're learning a few things. I'd like to have that anesthesia disappear." She said, "All right, now I can feel your hand on my knee again. I can move it," and she tested it. I said, "All right, I'm going to take my hand off your knee. How about developing anesthesia?" She said, "All right," and instantly she had the complete anesthesia. You can see what kind of a subject she was.

I said, "All right, now you need this medical procedure that's painful. Your husband can do it. You're a good hypnotic subject, you can develop anesthesia. Whoever has worked with you is impressed by your ability. What do you think the next time you go to the office, what do you think you'll do?" She said, "I know what I'll do. I'll go there full of good resolves. As soon as he gets ready to start, I'll lose my hypnosis, I'll lose my anesthesia." I said, "You're rather dignified, aren't you? You're a woman of strong opinions. *This* is what *you* are going to do. If your husband hasn't got a camera, he's going to get one." She said, "He's got one." I said, "Does he take color pictures?" "Yes." "All right. Your husband is going to take some pictures, and you aren't going to like them. They are going to be utterly, completely, ridiculously absurd and immodest. Unbelievably so. But you're going to do it. Because you've got two choices. One is to permit that medical procedure. If you don't, I want you – with the greatest of care, with absolute precision – I want you to braid your pubic hair into cute little pigtails." She said, "You don't mean this." I said, "Yes, I mean it. You braid your pubic hair in those tiny little pigtails. Your husband is to take colored snapshots of them, a whole row, and then you can take the film out of the camera and destroy it before it's developed." (Laughter) I said, "Call me tomorrow."

She called me the next day and said, "We've got the color film, but we're going to use it for other purposes entirely." (Laughter) A certain primness, a certain strength of character, a certain uncontrollable loss of her anesthesia.

H: This is an example of punishing them if they don't do something.

W: Well, it came up on the context of how do you get them to follow an instruction. And I don't know how you got her to follow the instruction that if she didn't go through the procedure, she would have to braid her hair that way and get the pictures taken of it.

E: How can you refuse to do such a completely idiotic, silly, ridiculous thing to an obviously ethical, professional man? You know, you just can't refuse.

H: You mean another way to get them to do something is to have them do something idiotic?

E: So completely idiotic, so completely out of context, something that nobody would ever ask you to do. (Laughter)

H: Well, not many people, that's right.

E: Just nobody would ask you to do a thing as silly as that. Then to take color snapshots of it, but destroy the film after the snapshots are taken. You see, the whole thing is so utterly, completely idiotically silly. Nobody in his right mind would ever ask it. Since nobody in his right mind would ever ask it, it's literally unasked and yet . . . (Laughter)

H: If nobody in his right mind would ever ask it, it's literally unasked?

E: The alternative to dealing with that *impossible* situation is to yield in the *current* situation.

H: Well, that's pretty similar to your curing the involuntary by the voluntary. By asking somebody to wet the bed.

E: Yes.

H: She preferred to keep the anesthesia rather than do that?

E: That's right.

H: Why did you involve her husband in taking the pictures? Why couldn't she take pictures of herself?

E: What would her husband say? What? (Laughter)

H: I can see how this could make it more so, I just wondered if this was also related to the fact that her husband was going to do this operation on her, or whatever?

E: Yes, well that's part, but you see it dealt with that situation so completely, asking her husband to do a completely futile thing, and she's turned it down.

W: I wonder if part of the reason she can't refuse to do this is that it's already come after the demonstration of how you can lay your hand on her knee. There's a very considerable demonstration there of how much she is in your power, but she can get out of it with the trance. I mean, maybe she had the idea if she doesn't braid her hair and her husband take this picture, my God, Milton Erickson is going to be over there doing it. (Laughter)

E: No, because I quite simply told her, "Of course you can refuse to do this." But I put my doubts into, "Of course you can *refuse* to do this." So I anticipated her on the refusal.

H: You mean you put doubt on the word "refuse"?

E: Of course she can refuse (with rising inflection on "refuse").

W: I'll bet she had some image of "What happens if I do refuse?"

E: But you see how intrigued would a person be by such an absolutely ridiculous situation. It's intriguing to you, isn't it?

W: Braids look very cute. (Laughter)

E: She's a good hypnotic subject. She's a very responsive person. Here's an intriguing, absurd, ridiculous, ludicrous – what does it do to a person? "Your idea is so silly that I think I'll accept it really." Why do you buy some silly cards – because they are so absurd.

W: And this was a lady of dignity?

E: Anybody with a great deal of dignity has to toy with the idea of complete absence of dignity. To make a colored snapshot record of absolute lack of dignity, and yet to destroy it before it's developed. Nevertheless, that doesn't abolish the fact that a record was made. If her husband is to be futile, let him be futile. (Laughter) The choice is between letting her husband be futile and letting her husband be successful. Of course, I'm the one that's going to know that her pubic hair was braided. I'm the one that's going to know. I'm going to share that with her husband. Is she ever going to let me know that she did? No, she was very careful to call me up the next day to tell me that the color film was going to be used for other purposes.

H: This would be between you and her husband for ever and ever in that case?

E: That's right. And she and she alone had the power to prevent it.

H: Do you know if she told her husband what you'd suggested?

E: Oh yes. She told him with a great deal of glee and amusement – after the medical attention had been given. You see. I'm disguising it.

H: Well, that's a real beauty!

E: She told me he leaned back in his chair and said, "I wish I had thought of that myself." He roared and roared with laughter. The word "braids" in some connection is now a standard family word. Always signifying something funny, absurd and ridiculous.

* * *

E: There's one particular point that I thought I would mention to you: That is the way I do certain things when I am interviewing a family group or a husband and wife or a mother and son. People come to a psychiatrist for help, but they also come to be substantiated in their attitudes. They also come to have face saved for them. Therefore, in dealing with them, I pay attention to the fact that they want face-saving, that they want to be substantiated; and I am very likely to speak in a fashion that makes them think that I am on their side. Then I digress on a tangent – one that they can accept, but it leaves them teetering on the edge of expectation. They have to admit that my digression is all right, perfectly correct. They didn't expect me to do it that way. But they're teetering there, it's an uncomfortable position; they want some solution of that matter that was just brought to the edge of settlement. Then they are much more likely to accept whatever you say. Because they are very eager then for you to make a decisive statement. If you made it right away, they could take issue, but if you digressed, they hope you will get back and they are wanting you to make that decisive statement.

Then there's another technique in presenting ideas. That is saying something so that they are forced to agree with you, to agree with you regretfully, to know that you're speaking the truth. They wish you wouldn't and then you give it a last, second flip, which compels them to accept it.

I can think of a wife who's the victim of a very paranoid husband. Her complaint was that he had never told her that she was attractive, but she was very charming. He always told her that lots and lots of women were more beautiful than she was, that practically every woman had as much or more charm than she. He said there was no possible way of giving his wife the type of compliment that she desired. My statement was that I could give his wife that sort of compliment deliberately, intentionally, and do it as a demonstration to him. His wife, sitting right there, hearing the discussion, would find herself unable to reject the compliment. So I turned to her and said, "You know, unquestionably there are many women more beautiful than you, but not for me." That admitted there were women more beautiful than she, but it also said she was the most beautiful woman in the world to *my* eyes. Now this woman has a Ph.D. She's highly intelligent. She examined that and said, "No matter what I try to do with that statement, I'm so pleased you made it." (Laughter)

That's right, you're admitting absolute reality, but you're transforming it into a purely interpersonal relationship reality which is genuine. So you're differentiating between the hard, harsh reality of the world in general, and establishing the reality of the interpersonal relationship world, which is of importance to the individual.

H: You have a way of presenting an idea in two steps so that the first step is impossible to disagree with. When you say, "Unquestionably there are women who are more beautiful than you are," the "unquestionably" is your first step. Then you follow it with a second. If they accept the first, they tend to accept the second.

E: Yes. You try to present the first step so that they can measure it in any number of ways, and it's still valid.

H: Well, I gather from that example, you would assume that if a wife protests that her husband doesn't pay her enough compliments, she's a wife who has difficulty receiving compliments. Would that be an assumption of yours?

E: No, that wasn't the assumption in this particular case. It was simply in the paranoid nature of the husband.

H: Do you assume that if he did pay her a compliment, she'd have trouble accepting it in that case?

E: Not in this case. But her orientation was one of wanting it only, only, only from her husband.

W: They were both there at the time you made this pair of statements?

E: Yes.

W: Then it was also in the nature of a demonstration to the husband that there are two kinds of reality?

E: That was part of it. His response was awfully nice. He said, "I wish I could have thought of it that way." But the next day he was just as paranoid against his wife as ever.

H: You tend to treat symptoms as if they had something to do with more than the one person with symptoms, but at the same time you tend to make them quite individual. I mean, you would assume, I think, with the paranoid man that his paranoia was independent of his wife.

E: Yes.

H: Instead of her being a part of it. Do you feel this is true of almost all symptoms, or just the psychotic sort?

E: It varies.

H: Let me put it this way. Do you think that a man of that sort could find a woman to live with who didn't need him to be that sort?

E: The paranoid system of this patient includes the whole wide world. I think the only role his wife is playing has been to slow him down in his delusional, hallucinatory developments.

H: You don't assume that she manages to be just secretive enough to keep him suspicious? That there's something going on that he doesn't get hold of? We find this fairly typical of a paranoid acting suspicious. He exaggerates the response, but there's usually something that he is responding to.

E: This man left his father and mother. He could not tolerate living at home because he was so filled with doubts and fears and suspicions of his parents. Then at a social party he saw a very attractive girl, and he inquired her name. He began investigating *her*. All of his investigations of her proved that she was a very nice girl. So with a great deal of relief, he started courting her. She was a nice, sweet, innocent, trusting girl.

W: I find that hard to believe.

* * *

H: When you see a couple who are fighting, do you ever analyze the tactics they use with each other?

E: Very, very often. I get a couple in here, the husband sitting there, the wife sitting there, and he starts telling her what kind of a liar she is, and she starts telling him what kind of a fool he is. I point out to the wife that she could have described him as a fool in much more eloquent terms. I point out to him that he could have described her in much more meaningful terms. I can also confess my absolute ignorance, "I don't know that you're going to go that far out."

H: Do you give them examples of how they could have done it?

E: Precisely. You get a nice, violent, verbal quarrel where obscenity and vulgarity and everything is included in the verbal descriptions. I know a few words myself that I think improve upon any profane utterances. Then I can confess that, "I don't know if you want to say all of that about your wife." I don't. What does it do to him? Well, does he want to say all of that? That's what I want him to start thinking. It's rather shocking to him to have me tell him how he could improve his denunciation. The words sound differently coming from my lips.

W: Yes.

E: Then, of course, I point out that I don't know if he wants to go that far in his denunciation. Well, of course, I am a third party, and I don't really understand, I've acknowledged that. But he's starting to think. I do the same thing to her. There you've got both of them thinking, "Do I really want to be that extreme in my utterances?" If they are quick enough in their responses, I can raise the question, "While we're dealing with this matter, I suppose you both want to disregard the favorable elements for a while." (Laughter) If they say, no, they don't want to disregard the favorable elements, they are committing themselves to the fact there *are* favorable elements. If they say they want to disregard the favorable elements for a while they are committing them . . .

H: That locks them in.

E: . . . committing themselves that there *are* favorable elements that must be touched upon before the fracas is over. But I haven't told them that there are favorable elements. I just raised a legitimate question.

H: Yes.

E: But it pushes their thinking around.

W: What if, instead of the couple having this sort of open fight, they are sitting there full of it, but not saying it.

E: Do you mean (demonstrating anger).

W: Yes.

E: Mouth shut, fists clenched.

W: "She's a fine woman," (said with mouth clenched).

E: I'll tell the woman, "Unquestionably you can read your husband's mind right now and you know the kind of things he's thinking. The kind of things that he hasn't got the courage to say, because I think it's lack of courage, I don't think it's courtesy. I think he's too darn mad at you to be courteous. Just as she is too darn mad to be courteous, and you can read the thoughts in *her* mind." Can he deny that he can read her thoughts? Can she deny? As long as the thoughts are open and readable, you might as well say them because they're out in the open anyway.

H: I gather that with couples you don't bring the couple in and get them talking to each other while you sit out of it at all?

E: Not very often. Once in a while.

H: Why do you do it that once in a while?

E: Sometimes to get a better view of the acidity of the situation. (Laughs) Just exactly how sour it is, you see.

H: Yes.

E: Just how bitter.

W: You know, I see something, Jay, where we tend to make a lot of that, but Milton brings them in and, in fact, revises them separately and sends them out to interact. Instead of having them interact in the room and trying to make a shift in it there. You send them out to go camping.

E: Yes. They come into the room to disclose their unhappiness. I send them out to establish their happiness.

W: And they can leave the other here.

* * *

E: When I talk to a wife and husband together, at times, the husband has the feeling, literally, that the wife and I are alone and he's an unknown, invisible, nonparticipating creature seeing what his wife and *I* talk about. I'm handling her that way. Then I have the wife observe the same thing about the husband. I can agree with the wife against the husband, and agree with the husband against the wife. Each feels that I'm in agreement with *them*. But all I'm doing is substituting the intensity of my interest for their wish for my conformity. Then I can take them as a marriage problem.

W: This really means that your interest in them is really more important than whether you agree with them or not.

E: That's right.

H: When you are involved this intensely with one of them, doesn't that one begin to feel that the other one is being left out and try to bring them in?

E: Very, very seldom because I don't allow that.

H: Of course. (Laughing)

E: I much prefer to have him sit there viewing it objectively even though it's not intentionally objective.

CHAPTER 5

Sex, Fun, and Impotency

1959. Present were Milton H. Erickson, Jay Haley, and John Weakland.

H: We were talking previously about something we would like to get back to. John was talking about an impotency case, and I have a premature ejaculation case. They are similar sorts of problems in that in both the emphasis is upon a crusade to give the wife some satisfaction. And you suggested that in these cases you tell them there will come a time when they will get an erection when it is inconvenient to the wife.

E: Yes.

H: Where do you go from there?

E: You see, what happens to their claim for impotence when they get an erection every time it's inconvenient for their wives?

H: Oh, it isn't that it is a single time, it's every time?

E: Over and over again. Not just one time. What has happened to their claim of impotence? This man with that phobia. What happened to his claim of a phobia for kissing his wife? When he kissed her when she was in the middle of washing her face at night, preparatory to going to bed. When he kissed her when she was in the middle of greasing her face. When he kissed her when she was going to take a shower preparatory to her dressing to go downtown for some function. When he insisted on kissing her when she was cutting her toenails, and things like that.

W: Well, would you repeat then just how you – you spoke earlier about how you had to phrase it to this man. I'd like to hear that again.

E: You want to know something about the thinking pattern of the person. Something about their speech pattern.

H: Okay. But to get back now. You have this man getting an erection at inconvenient times so he can no longer say the problem is impotency.

E: That's right. And we can both rejoice that we are nearer to the question, "And what is this very, very difficult problem that you had to conceal under the mistaken idea that you were impotent?" So you maximate the problem. You accept the erection. He's got to accept the erection in order to maximate the problem. He's again left the problem in your hands to be directed.

H: Do you do this with premature ejaculation too? That he would be able to maintain an erection when it was inconvenient for his wife? When she was too tired, or whatever?

E: I have another technique with the premature ejaculations. I point out to the man, "You know, it's really rather nice to have a premature ejaculation, because you see what you *can* do about it is just unload about a quarter of your supply of sperm. That can cut down your sensitivity, so that you're not overexcitable, and it will teach you the tremendously important thing of enjoying foreplay."

H: How does he unload a quarter?

E: I never explain any such impossible things. (Laughter)

H: And he doesn't ask you?

E: Oh no. "Well, it might be a third, you know."

H: If he does ask, you say that?

E: "It might be, you know." I'm not going to answer that impossible question. I give a new interpretation. I can think of a recent premature ejaculation case. He said, "Heck, I went to bed with a girl. Of course I had my premature ejaculation. But I thought over what you said about only a partial ejaculation. I realized, of course. I thought over what you said about how what I was missing by not having adequate foreplay, and I really explored that girl." Then he said, "Of course, just as you said, I had another erection and I really enjoyed it."

H: I see, it's the one-fourth, and then the foreplay, and then the erection again.

E: That's right.

H: The foreplay comes after the fourth.

E: That one experience literally cost me a patient.

H: How is that?

E: He isn't going to come back. He hasn't got any worries about premature ejaculation.

H: That's nice. I'll try that.

E: Oh, yes, then there's another approach. One of these long, long enduring cases of premature ejaculation, and that frantic, impotent attitude they take. I give a little song and dance in my most learned, erudite fashion, to the effect that there's always an unfortunate outcome with premature ejaculations. There is unexpectedly, one never knows when, usually after years – because my patient's told me it's been years he's been having premature ejaculations – usually after years, there will be a sudden reversal. And for the life of him, no matter how long he has intercourse, he can't have an ejaculation except upon a specific time realization.

H: What's a specific time realization?

E: That he starts having intercourse, and he expects to

have premature, but he doesn't, and that puzzles him and bewilders him. He inserts his penis, he really expects to have an immediate ejaculation, and he doesn't. That bewilders him and puzzles him and confuses him. He engages in active coital movements, momentarily expecting an immediate ejaculation, because it is so exciting and so thrilling and so satisfying. He keeps looking and looking and looking and looking and looking for an ejaculation that does not happen. After 15 minutes or 20 minutes or 25 minutes it suddenly begins to dawn on him that perhaps he has lost his capacity to have an ejaculation. Then he really begins to get scared because of the excitingness of the experience, and the enjoyableness of it. He's dead certain that all of that intense enjoyment ought to – and then he suddenly realizes, yes, he did wear his wristwatch, and that it was 9:00 o'clock when he went to bed with her, and that there is no possibility of his having an ejaculation, absolutely none of having one before 47 minutes past 9 o'clock, or till 7 minutes to 10, whatever time you want to set. You see, he's obsessed by the idea of premature ejaculation. All right, you let him get obsessed by the idea that he can't possibly have an ejaculation, until 47 minutes after the hour, or 7 minutes of 10. I don't care what hour you pick out. When the patient is having active intercourse, he insisted on having on his arm so he can see it, see his watch. (Laughter) Then he tells you all about it. You tell him that after a while – you don't know how long it will take him to learn – he'll learn to recognize time automatically, unconsciously, and he won't have to depend upon his watch.

W: You mean, he's being told, "Well, you can know when it's time."

E: That's all. Then you demonstrate how these people go to bed and they've got to catch a train at 6 o'clock. They wake up in full time for that.

H: How do you do this, when he's awake or when he's in trance?

E: Pretty much in a trance state. Maybe it's a light, maybe it's a medium, as well as a deep.

H: Now to get back to this question, what do you do after you make it so that it isn't a problem of impotency?

W: No, I want to go back one step before that. I got that, or at least I got part of that, but I don't quite get how you would get this across by, in effect, saying, "What you can expect is what you were concerned about before." That is, you say to the patient, "Yes, it's just sort of too bad that when you do begin to have an erection again it's going to cover all these inconvenient times, and that's going to be too bad. And your wife isn't really going to be ready for it, and therefore you are just going to have to expect that she is really not going to be satisfied, and this is too bad, but really that's the way it is."

E: Yes.

W: And having been told that, he begins to have an erection again and at an inconvenient time, and this leads into—well, this isn't really the problem.

E: That's right. But he's proved conclusively that he's competent to have an erection.

W: You've done it, really, by guaranteeing him that it is going to be inconvenient for his wife.

E: Yes, but you see he's making his recovery and he is getting closer to it. Now what happens when a man gets an erection?

W: I don't understand in what sense you are asking.

E: Doesn't he experience a few desires himself?

W: Yes.

E: That's been overlooked, you see. Nothing has been said about it. He's being frustrated too, you know.

W: Yes.

E: He still is during his erections. He's being frustrated. He can compromise and do it when it is convenient for his wife too. You're building up his desire. You're also giving him permission to inconvenience his wife. But you're building up *his* desires. You're making him aware of the fact that it isn't an inability to secure an erection. It's his attitude toward sexual relations in some way, but he's building up desire.

* * *

1955. Present were Milton H. Erickson, Jay Haley, and John Weakland.

E: A couple with a traumatic experience can reach an impasse. Let me give you an example. One of my medical students married a very beautiful girl. On their wedding night he could not produce an erection in spite of the fact that he had slept with every chippy in Detroit. For two weeks he tried to get an erection, and nothing could produce one. He couldn't even get one by masturbation. After two weeks of a honeymoon of that sort, they came back and his wife consulted a lawyer about an annulment. He came out to weep on my shoulder. I told him to call up a few of his friends who knew his bride and to get them to go and see her to persuade her to come out to see me. She came out just as bitter as could be. So horribly bitter. I let her tell me the whole thing. Then I asked her if she had thought about the compliment her husband gave her. She wanted to know what I meant. She had been completely in the nude, I pointed out, and said, "Well, evidently he thought your body was so beautiful that he was overwhelmed by it. Completely overwhelmed. And you misunderstood that and felt he was incompetent. He *was* incompetent because he realized how little capacity he had to appreciate the beauty of your body. You go into the next office and think that over." I called him in. I let him tell me the whole sad story.

And I said the same thing to him. How he had complimented his wife. They almost stopped the car on the way back to Detroit to have intercourse. A rather simple way of handling it, wasn't it?

H: Remarkably simple. Why do you think it worked?

E: Because on her wedding night every woman wants to be wanted, the one, the only, the absolute. Because it is a completely momentous occasion, representing her transformation from a girl into a woman. Now I built up the momentousness of that in the most pleasing way imaginable. It was an overwhelming situation, and she had proof that it was overwhelming. He had proof because he had a lot of guilt for sleeping with every chippy in Detroit. Here was proof to him that he had found the one, the only, the overwhelming one. You see, that became an irreversible thing.

H: It's just a different approach from what I am familiar with. I mean, the typical idea is that it's a problem of the good and bad girl, and it's not uncommon that as soon as you marry her you can't screw her because she's the good girl.

E: I know, but she wants to be.

H: It's a different way of handling it altogether.

E: What's the quarrel one of my patients has with her husband? It's so utterly bitter. "We can get along all right all evening; we've been married a year. But when we decide to go to bed, Joe gets an erection the second we start for the bedroom. I can undress slowly, or rapidly, he gets into bed with an erection. He has it every night. He wakes up in the morning and there it is standing up. It makes me so mad, and I'm getting madder and madder at him." I said, "What do you want?" She said, "If just once, just once, just once, he'd get into bed and not be able to have an erection no matter how much he looked at me and admired me. If just once he could let me feel my female power." Because every woman has the right to produce an erection and to reduce it.

H: That's a different view.

E: And she doesn't want the man just to produce it; she wants to produce it in him.

H: She's just "woman in general" if it's produced when he comes into the room, not her specific self.

E: She would like just once to feel her female power. So I swore her husband to secrecy, and I pointed out the tremendous importance of this. He masturbated three times that night. He really had a flaccid penis. She had a perfectly wonderful time wriggling around and squirming and so on, and he was wondering and wondering if he could have an erection. He knew what he wanted. After a while he got an erection. The thing that delighted her was that it was just by wiggling and squirming and never putting her hands on his penis and not even kissing him. He got his erection – she really had the female power.

H: I suppose they've been happy ever since then?

E: Yes. It's about time for them to fly over for a social visit. They took me out to dinner last April. Boy she's got female power. I was looking at her at the dinner table, and she's really got it.

H: Talk about unique methods.

* * *

1959. Present were Milton H. Erickson, Jay Haley, and John Weakland.

H: What do you do about the guy protesting that his wife is never satisfied? That this is the goal of his life – to satisfy his wife?

E: You want to know . . . you know my tendency to use analogies, and they work. If you went to a show, and it was a show you wanted to see very much. For example, there's the new Walt Disney film. Well, I am very interested in his natural history movies, very much so. And my sons are, and Betty is. I want to go and I want to enjoy that show, and I'm going to enjoy it with absolute intensity. But I'll swear at anybody who says, "Isn't that good? Isn't that good?" Do you want me satisifed? Let me alone. Let me enjoy it to the utmost. How are they going to enjoy the show if they see me enjoying it to the utmost? You go into a hotel, or a restaurant, you're not very hungry, and here is some uninhibited character really feeding his face with both hands with the greatest of gusto, and you say, "Well, I didn't realize I was that hungry."

H: So if you can get the husband to really enjoy it, the wife's problem will take care of itself?

E: You tell the husband that. And when he makes love with absolute gusto, what happens to his wife? Some of these frigidity problems, the husband said, "I tried to do everything in the world I can to make my wife enjoy it."

H: Yes, this is the problem we all see.

E: Yes.

W: He's working at it.

E: "You're enjoying it, aren't you?" No she isn't, that's right. But when she finds out that she is so completely, utterly, satisfying to *him*, that he just can't get enough of her (laughing), she has to think, "I must have something."

H: You explain this to him? Because it's hard to tell how much you explain to him.

W: How much you give him in analogy and how much you lay it out for him is not clear.

E: It's not clear because you can't let your patient—he wouldn't be your patient if he could handle it directly—know too much about it, or else he will consciously, deliberately improve upon your ideas. Therefore, you rely upon his unconscious.

W: And you've got to decide this for each patient, really is what you were saying before.

E: Remember, any six-month-old outsmarts its parents, isn't that right?

W: Quite often.

E: Quite often. I can think of the time when Kristina was three and little Stephani, her niece, my granddaughter, was two. And my daughter. We adults were sitting on the couch, and little two-year-old Stephani came in, saw Kristina's doll, grabbed it, and glared at Kristina as if saying, "I dare you to take this away." Kristina looked stricken. That was her favorite doll. She didn't want to have that strange little kid with her favorite doll. My daughter, Carol, Betty, and I were watching, wondering how the two little girls would settle it. Kristina said, "Please," reached her hand out. She turned away. Kristina thoughtfully scanned Stephani and turned and went into the bedroom and came out with a couple of tin cups with a saucer. Of course, Stephy watched Kristy, who sat down with her back toward Stephani and started rattling the cups and saucers. Stephani looked, Kristy switched around, Kristy just obstructed Stephani. Stephani threw the doll away on the couch and proceeded to show Kristy that she could take those cups and saucers away. So Kristy put up a mild, weak little struggle, and she kept reaching as Stephani backed away. As soon as Stephani was far enough away, Kristina picked up the doll, slipped it in her dress and walked blandly into the bedroom. She hid her doll and went back, and she weakly tried to take the cup again. Stephy shoved her away. Then Kristy went about her play. So I turned to my daughter, Carol, and I said, "When are you going to pay your fee on child guidance to Kristy?" Yes.

Now you watch any little child. I watch them in airports, maneuvering their parents. Kids in go-carts doing a beautiful job. It's important what a beautiful job they do. You'll see that nice, calculating narrowing of the eye, as a child thinks this over, "and now let's see, the old lady will fall for this." (Laughter) Then I watch mother being led by the nose by some little kid in the airport.

H: A little child shall lead them. (Laughter)

E: So when you deal with patients, you bear in mind that the unconscious is pretty childlike and pretty direct and pretty comprehensive in its understandings.

H: And you typically reach it with analogy?

E: It's the best way, I think.

* * *

E: This college professor in his 30s married a girl in her 30s. They met at a faculty meeting. He took one look at the girl and he *knew* that was the girl he wanted to marry, and how could he meet her? She took one look at him and knew that was the man she wanted to marry, and how could she meet him? So there was a desperate campaign on the part of both of them until they could really get introduced. They had a very warm courtship. They both asked during the courtship one specific thing: Did the other want children? And each did, tremendously so. They agreed that they would make a baby on their wedding night. They were rather prim and rigid and they used professional language. She wanted to know if he was phylopro-genital. He inquired about her maternal instincts.

They agreed that their wedding night should be for purposes of procreation. They agreed that it should be a very, very complete physical union, because there is something in psychosomatic medicine. There should be full participation emotionally, intellectually, and physically. On their wedding night they had intercourse and she had an orgasm, and so did he. Of course, one physical union does not necessarily result in impregnation. I'm just conveying their terminology. Therefore, there should be persistence, repetition. Since the time of ovulation is not necessarily known, they'd better have physical unions daily. Since the sperm cell lives not over 72 hours, probably less than 48 hours, it was only reasonable to have physical union daily. On the weekends to rest in bed, to caress one another, and to bring about psychosomatic responses and to culminate in complete physical union. Sundays and holidays twice a day. Weekdays, once daily. They were going to procreate. Oh yes, menstruation was not a barrier, neither was pneumonia, a broken leg, or anything. They never missed a day for three years. They both had orgasms.

At the end of three years they came to me rather desperate. They came with this pitiful story. They said, "The unfortunate thing is that in the desperateness of our desire to procreate we have become emotionally intolerant of each other. Our bodies function normally, but we're losing all of the tender emotions, and we look upon the physical union as just a hopeful labor and nothing else. Of course, we make it complete, we both have orgasms, maybe that's a superstitious idea about impregnation, but we feel it should be complete. But it's only a hopeful labor, and we're awfully intolerant of each other so far as tender emotions are concerned. We've both been examined. There's no reason why we should not become parents. But we've reached an emotional impasse, and we wonder if we'll be suitable parents for the child." Such rigidity, it was horrible.

I asked them what they wanted me to do. They

said, "Well, you're a psychiatrist. Maybe you can help us." I said, "Well, if you want therapy I *can* help you. But it won't be very pleasant, because you need shock treatment. Shock treatment that will really knock you into another kind of understanding. Not electric shock, not insulin shock, not metrazol shock, but an emotional shock. You're both very religious, you're both very conscientious, you're both very circumspect. You're both very refined. If you want therapy that will help you, I'll give it to you, but it will be a shock treatment. Do you want it? Think it over, wait awhile." They sat there and looked at each other, and turned to me.

I said, "Well, you've been having a physical union regularly every day for three years. Twice on Sundays and holidays. Whether sick or well, throughout the menstrual period. But why in hell don't you fuck for fun!" You should have seen them stiffen rigidly, holding their breaths. It was a shock. For me to say "hell" and me to say "fuck." Finally they took a breath. I said, "I mean that: Why don't you fuck for fun? Think of it. Why don't you fuck for fun?" I called the wife by her first name and said, "She has a pretty body, she's got nice hips, and she's got a nice breast, in fact she's got two, she's got twins. She's got nice legs, she's kissable and you know it. And as for you—and I called him by name—you know that you've got the thing that she can reduce in size. So why don't you fuck for fun? And for the next few months you'd better fuck for fun, and pray to God and hell that she doesn't get pregnant and interrupt your fun. Now get the hell out of here. Come back in a week or a month, and tell me how you're getting along. And remember that I meant everything I said."

I saw them about a month later. They didn't come to see me; I drove to their home. I walked in and told them I wanted a drink. So they fixed me a scotch and soda. The embarrassment on their faces. I walked around the house, took a quick look in the bedroom, grinned and said, "This is a delightful drink." I said I was driving by and thought I'd drop in. I was thirsty. Better sit around here an hour and let the drink wear off. How are things going in the department? So we discussed his teaching. I waited an hour for the drink to wear off. I think that was about a month afterwards. Then about three months later they came in to tell me she was pregnant. How does the body do a thing like that?

* * *

I can think of – let's call her Ann – she got engaged to a boy in the Air Force. She was going to marry him next December. In December she was going to marry him next June. In June she was going to marry him in December. In December she was going to marry him in June. In the meantime, she developed horrible phobias. She couldn't ride in a bus. She didn't want to go past a railroad station because of the trains there. She couldn't even go near an airport. She hated to get into a car. It was very troublesome.

But by aid of her mother coming with her, and her aunt coming with her, she came from Yuma, by car, all the way up here to see me. She told me she was in love with that boy up in North Dakota. She wanted to marry him. She showed me his letters. She was afraid, afraid, afraid, afraid, afraid. I had the boy write me a letter to find out what his views were on it. He was stupid enough to want to marry her. I thought she'd turn out all right if her horrible phobias were corrected, but I knew that would take quite some time.

The first thing I did was move her out of her maternal home. She could go back there on weekends. I made her move. A Spanish family. The grandmother really laid down the law to her, but I had laid down the law first. And somehow or another I was more effective than grandmother. Then this question of traveling. I told her to shut her eyes and *back into* the bus. (Laughs) She did. I don't know what the other passengers thought of that rather pretty girl, Spanish girl, with her eyes shut and backing into a bus. But she was so distressed about that that she didn't seem to realize that the bus was a means of transportation from Yuma to Phoenix. I later had her board a train backward. The conductor's cussing her out didn't seem to faze her one bit because the train was so horrible. Then I got her to ride in the back seat, looking out of the back window, from Yuma to Tucson to Phoenix to Yuma.

Then it was apparent – everytime the subject of sex was raised she developed deafness. She just turned blank. Apparently couldn't see you or hear you. So I told her the next time she came I wanted her to bring in, in her handbag, the shortest pair of short shorts imaginable and show them to me. Take them out of the bag and show them to me. She did. Then I gave her her choice in her next interview with me – she either walked in here wearing them or she put them on in here. (Laughter)

W: That's quite a choice.

E: She walked in with them. Then I told her, "Now you're going to listen to me when I discuss sex, or I'll have you take those off and put them on in my presence." She listened to me on the subject of sex. Then I told her, "Now this is the first of July; you've got until the seventeenth of this month to marry that guy. You're coming in tomorrow. I'm going to get you all ready to marry the guy. You've got to go on up to North Dakota and see him. Take a train. You've got to go up and meet his folks. You've got until the seventeenth of July. Come in tomorrow."

So I called Betty. I said, "Now you need to know how to undress and go to bed in the presence of a man. So start undressing." Slowly, in an almost automatic fashion, she undressed. I had her show me her right breast, her left breast, her right nipple, her left nipple. Her belly button. Her genital area. Her knees. Her gluteal regions. I asked her to point where she would like to have her husband kiss her. I had her turn around. I had her dress slowly. She dressed. I dismissed her. She went and bought a railroad ticket and went to North Dakota. Made all the arrangements with him to come down and marry her in Yuma. She sent me the wedding announcement. I could've been best man if I wanted to be. She broke the news to me so happily when she was first pregnant. Sent me an announcement of the birth of the first child, and an announcement of the birth of the second child. She's written me letters. After the birth of the second child she wrote me one of the nicest letters telling me how grateful she was that I had utterly disregarded social amenities and helped her.

And Betty sat here frozen-faced. But why did the girl do it? I expected her to do it. I thought it was utterly absolutely imperative; and if she didn't, she never could get to North Dakota. She never could marry the man. She could never get into bed with him. She says married life is wonderful, I'm very happy, and she married quite a wealthy young farmer. But you expect the patient to do it. Your patient is very certain that you know it's necessary.

Professor Arnt, Colorado School of Medicine, when I was an intern, was most emphatic in stating that sometimes the only way you can get a woman to consent to have an amputation of the breast for cancer, the only way you can get her to agree to it, is by stripping her to the nude and doing a very careful medical examination of her with your eyes. You ask her to walk, and then you tell her, "I'm very, very positive you need the amputation of that breast. I'm awfully sorry." And you are speaking against the total background of her nudity, her entirety. You can get some women, who would otherwise rather go to the grave, to enter the operating room gladly, hopefully.

This poor Spanish girl, you know how modest they are. Then I told her I thought it was necessary. Well, I did. Now with that four years of postponement of the marriage, those increasing phobias. The doctor in Yuma referred her to me and said, "You probably will have to put her in the state hospital." So I asked her to send him announcements of her marriage and her children. She's been back to Yuma with her family and visited the referring doctor.

W: How would you explain the working of that – what you did there?

E: That is something that you would never, never do for any, any man. Just never. Yet you've done it. Then anything else you do is necessarily much less; it's a minor thing. They've discovered that they can survive. You teach one of these extremely inhibited, completely fearful women who can't even say "darn," how to use the language of a longshoreman. And really use it. Then they can tell you, with utter simplicity, a lot of their fears and anxieties and conflicts that otherwise were too terrible ever to say. It may take a while – a whole hour to get them to say a few simple little four-letter words, but after that they can say almost anything. Their innermost secrets.

I can think of one patient who came to me and said, "You know, I wish I could tell you a few things." That was the burden of communication the first hour. The burden of communication of the second hour, "I really wish I could tell you some things." So for the third hour I said, "Do you mind if *I* take over now? I would like to have you spend," and I turned the clock so she could see, "the next 20 minutes silently, mentally, puzzling over the worst possible thing that you could say to me. The worst. I don't want you to say it. But you think over the worst possible thing that you could possibly say. You have 20 minutes to do it. You need never tell me what it is." I watched her face, and at the end of 20 minutes I said, "Now, you've thought it over. What is the worst possible thing that *your husband* has ever said about you, that you just wouldn't want to tell me?" She told me. She said, "We were out in a restaurant, you know the other couple," and she named them. "My husband was talking to her husband, and it was a crowded restaurant. There were people there who knew us. My husband always talks in a loud tone of voice, and he told her husband, 'All my wife is is a cold-assed broad.' And then her husband said, 'So is my wife a cold-assed broad.'" Now, that was the worst possible thing her husband could say. I've had no further difficulty; she can say anything and everything to me. It was probably something very mild. (Laughter) But you see, you set it up that way, and then you shift the entire setting – the worst possible thing *you'd* say, the worst possible thing *the husband* ever said about you. She resents being described in those terms. Her husband needs an awful lot of therapy. Both of those husbands do. Because I know them both.

H: You do a lot of shifting context. You get a context clearly defined, and then you take them clear outside of that.

E: Oh yes.

W: Leaving their resistance behind.

H: Yes.

E: Well, what does a good prizefighter do? He always gets the other fellow to think, "He's going to sock me on the nose." And he gets a body blow. Then he gets the other fellow to start defending his body, and he gets clipped in the eye. Well, that's right. In therapy your patient is going to offer you resistances of all kinds. Well, you ask them to put that resistance in a certain place. Where it's handy, where it's ready, where it's useful. He sort of keeps his eye on it right there where he can use it. And you walk around. But he did come to you for help, and you keep stepping under his guard by that shift of context. I never try to take a nice, systematic history. I always take a fragmentary history. You get much, much more information. The patient comes in prepared to tell you because they've seen other doctors take a nice orderly history. They also come in prepared to omit certain things, and that's on their mind. So you jump to something else.

W: They've got it organized so that if they give it their way, the omissions won't show too much.

E: Yes. And you jump to something else. The first thing you know, there's a great big hole, obviously. Another great big hole. So you go down the list. I can think of one patient. I said, "You lived in New York all your life. You had a boyfriend in 1919, and the next in 1923, and your next boyfriend was 1929, and apparently you didn't have any jobs in between 1923 and 1929, and apparently you weren't living in New York in that length of time. Because I did ask you for the periods of time which you lived in New York and when you lived elsewhere. You've given me your history, but there's this great big period of time, six years." She said, "That was what I wasn't going to tell you." I said, "All right, think it over carefully. Now what part of that six years don't you want to tell me?" I gave her a chance to hold out. She held out 1927, told me all the rest. Then she said, "You know, I might as well tell you 1927 anyway."

H: One question here that we haven't touched at all: Is there any sort of a psychiatric problem that you don't think could be resolved without involving the spouse?

E: Without involving the spouse?

E: There are a lot of problems where you are going to have to deal with the patient where the spouse won't come in.

H: But is there a problem that couldn't be resolved without bringing the spouse in, that you can think of?

E: Well, you hear about personal problems, purely personal, that interfere with the adjustment to the spouse. I can give you an example. This college professor came in to see me. In essence, he had never had an orgasm. He had never had an ejaculation. He had looked up the word "ejaculation" in every dictionary. He had quizzed a lot of people about it. But he came to me to find out why the word "ejaculate" was used in relationship to male sexual behavior. So I asked him immediately, "How long did you wet the bed?" He said, "Until I was 11 or 12 years old. I got over it then, and what's troubling me is my sexual problem." I said, "Well, you say you don't know what the word 'ejaculate' means. You've had intercourse with your wife. You've got two children. Your wife is happily married, you say. What do you do instead of ejaculate?" He said, "Well, you have intercourse, you enjoy it, and after a while, just as if you were urinating, the semen flows out of your penis." That's right. I said, "Well, you learned in your childhood that all your penis was good for is peeing. You've resented it. You've been ashamed of it. So in the use of your penis maritally, you used it to pee the semen into your wife's vagina." He said, "Doesn't every male?"

I told him what he ought to do is to say nothing to his wife at all, but every day, or every other day, he should reserve an hour for himself, go into the bathroom, and masturbate. In the process of masturbation, identify all the parts of his penis. From the base to the glands, identify all the sensations. That he should try not to pee semen as long as possible to see how excited he could make himself while masturbating himself. What little touches, thrills that he could add to the masturbation. And do it every day. The things of concern would be the sensation of warmth and friction, the tension, but not the peeing of semen, hold off on that, because once you've lost the semen, there will be a loss, physiologically, of the capacity to continue masturbating. Spend an hour doing it.

Well, he thought that was awfully childish, awfully foolish, and so on, but he did it regularly for about a month. Then one night at 11 o'clock he called me up and said, "I did it." I said, "What do you mean?" He said, "Well, instead of masturbating today I went to bed tonight with my wife and I got sexually excited and I *ejaculated.*" He said, "I thought you'd be glad to have me call you and tell you about it." I said, "I'm very happy that you had an ejaculation." At 1 o'clock he called me again. (Laughter) He'd had another. Now, there was therapy without the spouse being involved, and yet the spouse was, in a way, involved. His wife demanded to know why he called me up to tell me he had intercourse with her. So he brought her over and asked me if he should tell her. I told him it was none of her gol-danged business. But I'd like to ask his wife a few questions. So I asked her, "Have you enjoyed your marriage with your husband?" Yes she had. "Your sexual life has been good?" She said, "Yes." Sometime later she came to see me and said, "You questioned me about my sexual life, and I told you it was good. Ever since my husband called you up at midnight to tell you he was making love to me, my sex life with him has been better, but I don't know why."

* * *

1961. Present were Milton H. Erickson, Jay Haley, and John Weakland.

H: Do you give explicit instructions to the husband on how to handle his wife? I can think of a husband, for example, who complains that his wife would answer the phone, and if it was for him, she would ask who it was. If the person wouldn't say, she'd hang up. He treats this like this is just a way of life.

E: I don't think I'd give the husband instructions. I think I'd give the wife instructions.

H: What sort in that sort of a situation?

E: It would be a roundabout way of pointing out to her the essential integrity of the self. There are certain things that the individual must keep a secret from other people. There is no reason why a wife would announce to her husband that her first menstrual day has begun. It's of importance to him, but still that's a private personal thing. That the contacts that one makes – there are so many contacts that one should keep a secret. Why should husband keep his contacts secret? I don't think any woman should train her husband never to keep from her the secret of his Christmas present to her. The secret of his birthday present. The secret that he is having his sister-in-law quietly buying a desired Christmas present or birthday present. That the neighbor's wife has called him up because the neighbor's wife is chairman of the committee instructed to be sure that his wife is present at a certain church meeting so that she can be elected president of the group.

I think there are lots and lots of secrets. Secrets are essential for the integrity of one's own living. We even keep secrets from ourselves. Which is your right thumb and which is your left thumb? Are you right or left thumbed? How many men actually know which trouser leg they put on first? How many women know that certain blouses they button here down, and other blouses they button this way? They don't know it. But that different approach is vital to their appreciation. You see, this idea of having a full and comfortable knowledge of everything means that you may have a full knowledge but you can't have a comfortable knowledge.

The illustration I've given to various medical societies is this: You see a very, very lovely girl, an extremely kissable girl, and you'd really like to kiss her, and you'd really like to hug her. But then you notice her eyes are just a little bit close together, and her ears really do stick out just a trifle. That nose is a millimeter or so too long, and the upper lip is a bit thin and a bit short. The chin is slightly heavy. The first thing you know the girl *isn't* kissable. You reverse that.

I was sitting in the airport and I saw the homeliest girl I ever saw in my life. It was just incredible what her face looked like. So I thought, well, I've picked pretty girls' faces apart, now let's see what happens here. She had a very lovely widow's peak. That hairline was worth seeing. She had beautifully shaped eyebrows. The look, the expression in the eyes, was such an awfully nice, soft and gentle expression. Her ears were remarkably well-shaped. A very lovely lobe, and nice contours of the ear. Her nose, when you just looked at the nose separately, was really a nicely, well-chiseled nose. That upper lip had a beautiful cupid's bow. She was definitely kissable.

You give that illustration to people to enable them to recognize what they can do by over-analysis. You say to a woman, "Now your husband represents another sex. Another biological structure. Another biological significance. Another type of biological learning. Since your child has to live in a world of men and women, be sure you get the benefits of that, but don't try to pick that husband apart into component items, fragments." This makes it her responsibility, in her dominance, to provide everything, including a significant husband. You get her to be aware of the folly of picking things apart. You see, once you can get a cancer patient to start picking his pain apart, you have done a great deal toward relieving that sense of pain. It's a most effective measure.

W: You get them to sort of dissect it for you?

E: Yes. You dissect the pain, the locality, and is it hot, cold, cutting, biting, burning, lacerating, stabbing, grabbing, nagging pain? (Laughs) As soon as he starts in on each of those adjectives, he's beginning to look at the different things. You see, a pain experience depends upon the stimulation of, I don't know how many, nerve fibers, each of which presumably carries a slightly different sensation, and the pain is the composite experience. You get a great deal of attention on the hot, burning pain, and the cold, hard, drops out. Every patient who tries to describe pain to you, if you give them an opportunity, they'll throw in plenty of adjectives. I use that understanding in knowing that a woman should look at her husband and not pick him apart, but she better recognize his biological entirety.

W: When the individual patient is relieved of a problem and improves, do you think the spouse tends to develop some difficulties? And how is this dealt with? I have the feeling, from what you've been saying, that you start to deal with it in the beginning, but let's go on anyway.

E: Yes. Another example is when the alcoholic quits his drinking, and the wife no longer has a chance to nag him. Well, when he first comes to you, and his wife comes to you in the initial meeting, that's one of the questions you're going to put to them right away.

W: What form are you going to put that question in?

E: I let the husband define the situation. "I don't think I'd be an alcoholic if she didn't nag me all the time." My question would be to the wife, "I doubt if you really nag him, I expect you express your legitimate regret that he drinks excessively, and that has used a lot of your energy in the past. As he improves, just what are you going to use that energy for?" I have her wondering about it. But he has got an opportunity of suggesting to her, and watching and seeing to it, she uses her energy on those other areas. He has to stop drinking in order that she'll have that energy to use in other areas. You see, you always tie the two in together. But you never tell them that. Very rarely do they see through it. But when you commit her to using her time and energy elsewhere, you're committing him to giving her the opportunity.

W: Putting it in terms of energy makes it positive and carries a suggestion something good can be done with this.

E: Yes. You point out, "Each morning you wake up with a certain allotment of energy. During the day you'll use it up. By bedtime you'll be tired. You want to go to bed and replenish your supply of energy. How are you going to spend that energy during the day?"

W: Well, when you see a patient with a reasonably severe symptom, do you assume that if he improves, there's going to be a reaction in the family that you have to take into account?

E: Usually there *is* a reaction. The alcoholic – I asked his wife, I asked his daughter or son, "When father ceases to be an alcoholic, just how are you going to spend that time that you spent in the past devoting your energy to wishing he wouldn't, or avoiding him, or hammering away at him that he better mend his ways? How are you going to spend that energy?" I've had school children say, "Well, I can put it in on my geometry." I've had a wife say, "Now I'll have a chance to do some committee work at the church."

H: Sometimes you see this sort of a problem, that a very severe symptom can appear to be quite protective with the spouse. For example, if you get somebody who is afraid he's going to die of a heart attack, he's likely to have a depressed wife. The more he identifies himself as the patient, the more her problems don't come into the picture. As soon as he begins to improve, then she tends to get more depressed.

E: Now who has the bad heart?

H: The husband.

E: The more he improves, the more depressed she gets. Because she's lost her usefulness in this time of crisis.

W: I'm not sure you made it clear that this heart attack isn't a heart attack.

H: That's right. It isn't a real heart attack. I'm talking about hysterical . . .

W: This guy has a heart attack two or three times a week, doesn't he?

H: Well, the particular one I'm thinking of, and I think it's common with a lot of other symptoms, is a man who fears he's going to die of a heart attack. He has had 15 doctors tell him he's not going to die of a heart attack, nothing is wrong with his heart. So in the morning he says to his wife, "I think I'd better stay home today. If I go to work, I'll have a heart attack." She gets mad immediately. Or he takes his pulse, and this makes her furious. As I look into it, his wife is a very depressed looking woman. About the second session or so, when he began to improve, what came up was her suicidal inclinations. It's almost a picture of her getting depressed and him not knowing what's going on with her. He starts to protest that his heart feels so bad. She then gets angry and starts to talk, and he gets a better idea of what state of mind she's in, even though he gets her furious. Then he feels a little better later and they get together again. It's hard to tell what starts the heart business, but it's a kind of a system that the more he has the heart business, the more depressed she gets. The more depressed she gets, the more worried he gets and needs the heart business in order to find out what's on her mind.

E: My tendency would be to introduce – what would you call it? – vengeful anger.

H: How do you mean?

E: I can think of that man who dominated his wife with his threats of heart attack and dying, and his moaning and groaning, and so on, regularly. In spite of the doctors' all saying there's nothing wrong with his heart. It's such a useful way of making life miserable for his wife. I told her to get advertising material from every mortician in town. And say, "Oh, your heart *is* bad." She got advertisements and scattered them all around the house. Every time he mentioned his heart attack, she would say, "Now I must pick up those from that table and arrange them neatly." She was looking at this collection of ads from morticians. He would irately throw them away, but she had others. He didn't dare to mention it. But you see, that's vengeful behavior. "You're hurting me, you're annoying me, you're doing it deliberately. What's sauce for the goose is sauce for the gander." She varied it by adding up his insurance policies. She got advertisements for perpetual care and everything else. She would say, "Well, you need a good ride out in the fresh air; let's go see such and such a cemetery." She really had a very vengeful time, and he quit it. The wife would walk over to the telephone, dial the building contractor in her husband's presence, and say, "I hate to bother you again, but do you think you can get the house finished before my husband dies?" He got so that he grabbed that receiver out of her hand and would tell the contractor, "This is a wrong number." He was furious at me for telling his wife what to do. He said he didn't like that. Nevertheless, he sent me other patients. Oh, about a year and a half later he called me up to ask me how long he ought to spend in Florida away from his work. I pointed out to him that he was a grown man, his wife was a grown woman, and their son was a grown man. That he had enough money so he didn't need to work anymore. He should stay in Florida until the pleasures and satisfactions palled.

W: That's how to give him advice. He asks you, but you put it back to him anyway at the same time.

E: All at the same time. And you define the situation. The man was decidedly wealthy.

* * *

E: I can think of the husband and wife. The husband said his wife was way out in left field. She said maybe she was, but there were a number of things that made her think she wasn't, that it was her husband who was out in left field. So I asked her which one should begin first. She said, quite sharply, "I think my husband is way out in left field, he thinks I am; therefore, I'm going to let him talk first, and he'll say a lot of foolish things that he would be too wise to say if I spoke first."

So her husband did speak first. He pointed out that his wife was so unreasonable, so psychotically apprehensive and fearful of poverty that she objected to his having any recreation. His recreation was puttering around the old car, washing the engine, shifting the tires, cleaning off the greasepan, fixing up the spark plugs. He enjoyed that every weekend. His wife objected to spending time that way. You could see his wife sitting there getting madder and madder, until I asked the appropriate question. I said, "The fixing of the *old* car, that means then you've got two cars. Because you differentiated them. One is the 'old' car." I said, "How old is the 'old' car?" This was in 1960. He said, "Well, I bought it in 1948." I said, "All right, and you spend weekends working on it, fixing it up. How many weekends have you driven it?" He said, "I haven't got it all put together yet." Twelve years. I said, "About how much did you spend in the way of replacements and new things?" He said, "Not over $3,000." Then I asked him what he thought his wife crabbed about. "Because I have a little recreation, she crabs." And what does she want for recreation? "She'd like to go for a drive in the car." Twelve years fixing up that one car.

W: Keeping her dangling on the string for the ride forever.

E: Yes. I asked him if that wasn't a bit too long to spend on a car? He said, "No." I saw his wife later and she said, "Well, my husband is a good provider. He does waste a lot of money on that car, but he doesn't chase out with other women. He doesn't get drunk. He works steadily. He doesn't give me much pleasure in life, but I do have a good home, plenty to eat, plenty to wear. I think I'll quit fighting with him about the car, and let that little boy keep right on. I'm going to look after my *own* personal pleasures, just as he's looking after *his* own." There's really no sense in talking to the man; 12 years to fix up the second car, spending $3,000 on it. He had an altimeter on it. (Laughter) Not on the family car though. But for 12 years he's been building and rebuilding.

W: You wouldn't think he'd need any gauges at all for a car that never got out of the garage. Let alone an altimeter.

E: His wife abided by the fact that she would never get a ride in that car.

H: Do you know if he ever finished the car?

E: A year later – let's see, it was last January, I checked with her – he was ordering a new set of a different kind of fenders.

CHAPTER 6

Metaphors, Shocking Experiences

1959. Present were Milton H. Erickson, Jay Haley, and John Weakland.

H: One of the things we touched on the other day is how you manage to start a fight between a couple who isn't fighting and who ought to have a fight. You mentioned a couple ways to do it; we just wondered if there are other ways.

E: Except to ask them directly.

H: Well, usually they're unable to if you do that. You get a couple who say, "We've never had a fight. Married 23 years and never had a quarrel." They look upon fighting as something that isn't the sort of thing that ought to be done.

E: Yes.

H: Therefore, anything they object to about each other, they never say what it is. They go through life side by side without really contacting each other because they don't have a fight, really.

E: They tend to be a pretty colorless couple. What can you do with them? Their kids are going to be pretty colorless too. Unless, in some way, one of the kids blows up and then he becomes delinquent. I've sometimes made the approach, "If you were a *less* tolerant woman, if you were a *less* tolerant man, what do you suppose would be the things you'd disagree with about your spouse?" I don't know of anything else to add to that point.

H: With the husband who followed his wife around while she did the housework, you suggested that one way to start a fight is to do something absolutely absurd.

E: Yes.

H: Such as spreading the dirt around for him. I thought that maybe there were other tactics that you assumed were ways to start a fight.

E: The introduction of anything that is incomprehensible – *anything* that's incomprehensible. If you want to pick a quarrel with your associates, with your kids, with your wife, use that technique of doing something utterly incomprehensible. Ask the child to polish your shoes, the child gets all through, you deliberately slop water on them, and foolishly say, "It spots them, doesn't it?" That total feeling of being at a loss is a very disagreeable feeling. "Will you sew this button on for me?" Reluctantly done. So after it's done, you say, "It really was tight, wasn't it?" and tear it off.

H: Well, that's both undoing what was done and being incomprehensible.

E: Yes. You see, it's a destructive thing. Like, perhaps this will illustrate a point, I went into a hotel dining room. The menu was in French. The waiter showed off his knowledge of French to me. I said rather simply, "I don't understand French. I don't speak French and I don't read French. What is this item?" He poured out a string of French to me. I repeated, and asked him again, and he poured out French to me. My feeling was, "Brother, this is your misfortune." I said, "Will you get me a glass of ice water please?" "Oui, oui." Then I told him that I would like a bottle, about this high, of French dressing. He looked puzzled, "Oui, oui," and brought me the bottle. I dumped some French dressing in the ice water and said, "Take it out." He said, "Yes sir." (Laughter) I got nothing but English the rest of the time. But you see, that is fight picking, only I had all of the advantage.

H: One of the problems we run across, since we noticed that there's a reaction in the spouse if the patient improves, is how to get the spouse to cooperate in doing something that will bring about some improvement. You seem to be able to get the wives and the husbands to do what you want them to do. For example, I remember once when we were here, you had an alcoholic whose wife took away all his clothes because he took a drink. We were wondering how you manage to get the spouses to do this sort of thing with such full cooperation.

W: They don't always seem to us to be the most cooperative people.

E: I don't know. You ask the people to do it, and you ask it of them in such an utterly simple, expecting way that they have no way . . .

H: It's related to the similar problem of getting *any* patient to do anything, isn't it?

E: You simply assume. You know they're going to do it. They have the feeling that you know they're going to do it, and what can they do about it?

W: You expect them to do it, but you don't expect that they're going to want to do it?

E: Oh no.

W: You just expect that it will be performed.

E: It's going to be done. I can think of this patient in particular. I told her that since she was raising a row about her cardiac condition, I'd have Mrs. Erickson come in and sit down and chaperone while I examined her heart. That I would ask Mrs. Erickson to be very courteous, not to smile or be amused, because of her reluctance about taking off her blouse. And especially about her reluctance about taking off her bra, and especially her argument that she didn't need to take both sides of the bra off. You see the progression there? Because she was looking forward to the argument that it wasn't really necessary to take off the right side of the bra. Because the row about the blouse was only a preliminary to the bra. The bra is only a preliminary to this part. In order to get to this part she had to dispose of those preliminaries.

W: Well, you cut the ground out from under a whole lot of this in the beginning by saying you'll instruct your wife not to laugh at this.

E: That's right.

W: This labels it as pretty fantastic in a way she can't object to, since you're protecting her.

E: Yes. I'm protecting her. So Betty came in and sat down with a deadpan expression. The patient said, "Mrs. Erickson, you aren't going to let him make me take off my blouse?" And I said, "She's here as a chaperone, not as a source of information or comment." Well, that's true. "You can listen through my blouse." "But I don't want to." I said, "Take it off, and take off your bra." She got her blouse off, and she held her bra and unfastened the back of it, and she insisted, "But I don't have to take that off." I said, "I told you take off your bra so I could listen to your heart." She said, "Yes, all right." I said, "That's as much as I asked you to do, isn't it?" I wasn't arguing about holding this here (in front of her). She had taken off her bra so I could listen to her heart. How much *off* would it have to be? So she won a certain point, but I won my entire point.

W: Oh I see.

E: Then I told her, "Now the next time I will probably want you to do calisthentics with your arms while I am listening to your heart." (Laughter)

W: I begin to get the impression you're working on some things here.

E: Yes. You see, she felt relieved that I didn't ask her to do that this time. She felt relieved about my listening to her heart. She also resolved I wouldn't have to listen to it again and so improved. You always give your *relief* when you order a patient to do something that they don't want to do.

* * *

W: One of the things we are concerned about is how you choose when you will see only one person and work on a situation, and how you decide when it is more important to see more than one member involved in something.

E: Well, in private practice you have to do it the way the patient is willing to have you do it. You always try for what you think is the most comprehensive and the best, recognizing that maybe you're not going to get any cooperation. You always try to find out from your patient just how the other person at home reacts. The other person will try to probe and find out what happens in the therapy. Sometimes you feed the other person's curiosity. You say to a woman, here and there, that you don't know just how her husband would feel about such and such. It is something she can mention to her husband. Her husband has got to formulate what he is told. He's got to decide how to think about it. The next time she'll tell you how he responded, and you can reconstrue his utterance. The first thing he knows, he's beginning to recognize that he has got to come in and straighten you out on a number of things. (Laughter) So he insists that his wife make an appointment for *him*.

H: You make it clear to the wife that this is all right with you—if this should come up in the future?

E: I make it very clear at the beginning. "I think I can do therapy with you satisfactorily if your husband does not come to see me. But I'd like to have it clear that I'll be delighted to see your husband any time he wants to see me." That's already set up and may be repeated again. A wife had been in therapy for five years with an analyst. Three hours a week. The husband brought his wife to me saying, "I'm sick and tired of paying fees three times a week for five years. My wife is worse off now than she was when we started. There's nothing wrong with *me*. Everything belongs to my wife; she is the patient. So I'm not going to see you again, and I want that clearly understood." He was most emphatic.

I saw his wife – what was it – about seven hours, I think. Each time I fed her a statement, on some minor point, which would be at variance with his attitudes. "I don't know how your husband would feel about this particular subject, what his beliefs and understandings are." He always pumped her about every interview, and she always told him that.

After about seven hours he gave her orders to make an appointment for *him*. He came in and said, "I want you to shut up. I'm going to tell you the therapy that should be done with my wife." I said, "You're going to tell me the therapy." He said, "Yes, and shut up." I said, "Well, let me say a few things more. You're going to tell me the therapy, and I'm very glad you are. Will it be all right if I keep the notes I have on the case, which also outline the therapy that should be done?" He said, "Of course, you can keep your notes." He outlined exactly the things *I* was going to recommend.

Now this is a marriage – 17 years ago this very nice, sweet, gentle, maternal Mormon girl married this charming, attractive Irish lad. Her ambition – to have a houseful of Mormon children. Before he married her he wanted her to understand that he didn't want to father any child that lived as hard a kind of life as he had lived in his parental home. Therefore, as a preliminary to marriage he was getting a vasectomy. She married him, knowing he had a vasectomy. He was almost immediately called into service overseas. Well, with a vasectomy you run no risk. He wrote home to his parents that he wanted his wife to move in with them, and that they were to keep watch over her. She spent a miserable three years living with his parents. She couldn't go down to the corner grocery in broad daylight without being chaperoned. His parents didn't like her for marrying their boy. She stayed with them for three long years. He came back and accused her of every indiscretion imaginable. He said, "A woman is to be used by a man, that's all."

For 17 years they've been like that. They've built up a half a million dollar business together. They've got ability. They have worked from 6 in the morning to 10 at night, hard. All they've got is that half a million dollars worth of business. That daily, bitter quarreling, the nasty things he says about her. She gets even with him. Every Sunday he drives her to the Mormon church. He hates the Mormons. He sits in the car outside the Mormon church waiting for her to get through. For five years they talked to that analyst about – he used to go regularly to the analyst also – about separation, voluntary, legal, or divorce.

So I had a joint interview with them. I told him, "You sit there and you keep your mouth shut." To the wife, I said, "and you sit there and you keep your mouth shut. I'm going to summarize this entire thing." I did it essentially the way I have with you except with much more detail. I said, "Now, you've come to me for therapy, for advice and consultation. It doesn't make a bit of difference to me whether you keep on fighting the rest of your lives or not. It won't make any personal difference to me if you have a voluntary separation or a legal separation or a divorce. You don't have to get any one of them, but if you want any therapy from me, you're going to do one of those three things: voluntary separation, legal separation, or divorce." They both said, "This is what we should have been told five years ago." I said, "I'll give you an appointment in a week's time. At that time you'll tell me what you're going to do. Then I'll know when I'm going to see you again." I asked him what he thought of himself, marrying a Mormon girl who had wanted children and, as an engagement present, giving her a vasectomy. I asked her what she thought of herself, giving him as a wedding present a frustrated wife.

W: I think this covers the point I was about to raise because in this case it certainly would seem that, while in some overt respects he was a difficult character, she certainly was going along with it.

E: She matched him kind for kind. He gave her an engagement present of a vasectomy; she countered with that wedding gift, a completely frustrated wife. And 17 years of hammering it home to each other. I'm going to be interested in what they say next Tuesday.

H: What decision they'll make? What do you predict?

E: I ran through the essential details. There are living quarters at their place of business. Now they own a residence right alongside of it. I pointed out that if they had a separation or a divorce, it would have to be genuine. One of them should live at least two miles away from the business. One of them should live in the living quarters of the business, as a watchman. A caretaker during the night. I pointed out to them something they already knew – their business is frequently broken into. They already know that. I thought the man should stay in the living quarters in the business. I thought she ought to go elsewhere and have an apartment. As long as the business was furnishing his living quarters, the business ought to furnish hers. Whenever he needed therapy, he ought to come to me. Whenever she needed therapy, she ought to come to me. Let the business pay for that. And even-steven each take a modest salary from the business.

H: Well, is your goal to get them to separate?

E: Yes.

H: And then to go back on better terms, or a real separation?

E: I told them I thought they ought to separate in an absolutely genuine fashion for six months at least. Maybe they would discover a craving for each other, or they might discover an honestly-based hatred. I didn't care which, as long as they really discovered their true feelings. I pointed out to them a voluntary separation is cancelable at any time. A legal separation is cancelable at any time. As for a divorce, you can always remarry. No trouble at all – a two-dollar license fee.

I've urged a couple to go down and get divorced, being perfectly willing to bet that they would remarry, but on a different basis. They didn't know that when they got the divorce. But unless they take some kind of action, they won't discover.

I told a patient, "You and your lawyer are going to insist on a court trial for that divorce, and you're going to fight it to the bitter end. Your husband's going to fight it to the bitter end. The amount of bitterness in your husband is just unbelievable. And he's completely unscrupulous. He's so very unscrupulous that he won't give a darn about the judge. I would advise you to tell your lawyer to settle it out of court, because I don't see how any judge is going to permit it to be settled in court." So yesterday – the case began on Monday, Tuesday, Wednesday – on Thursday afternoon the judge said, "I'm interrupting the procedure. Speaking from the bench, this case is to be settled out of the court. It's going to be settled out of court, or I am going to render a decision that will be unpopular with both parties." The man overplayed his hand, as I knew he would. I've had him in this office. I think I know what the judge is going to say. "There's a million dollars at stake here. Your wife wants half of it. She wants part of your estate tied up for the benefit of your son. I think the right thing to do is to put your estate in trust for your son."

W: Take it out of both their hands.

E: Because the father was insisting that he loved his son, the mother was insisting she loved her son. I think the judge saw a wide, wide opening. But I knew that father. Good heavens, having him here in this office and letting him rant and rave. He's one of these advertising dentists who's absolutely unscrupulous. With a tremendous drive. He's working in a dental office, promising new patients everything imaginable. Advertising, and he's working in his office 20 hours a day. Now he's got a staff of I don't know how many dentists. He's been keen on his investments. You should be willing to tell a patient certain things, whether they like them or not, to get them to understand that it is a matter of medical judgment. I despise those physicians who tell a patient with cancer of the breast that it's a tumor, probably benign.

* * *

E: A patient of mine decided to divorce her husband. She brought in a lawyer friend who was also a friend of her husband. She said, "He has something to say to you." The lawyer said, "For what reason are you urging my good friend to get a divorce from her husband, who is also my good friend?" I said, "Start thinking like an attorney. Look over the past years, think of all the things that you, as an attorney, would employ to further a divorce suit. Keep telling them to me." It took him only 40 minutes to turn to my patient and say, "You come to my office on Monday and sign the papers."

When he left, I turned to my patient and said, "Keep that appointment. He'll draw up the papers for you to sign. Then ask him this one question, and you will know what to say when he answers." She did that, asking him, "When are you going to file these papers?" He said, "In a couple of days, a week or so." She said, "Today." So he did.

She brought him in later, he didn't know why. I said, "You've drawn up the papers and filed them. What arrangements have you made for the community property? I think you better investigate, as an attorney. My patient says that her husband owes $200,000 in spite of the fact that the famous restaurant he manages made large profits the last four years. He pays himself a handsome salary. My patient inherited some money from her father. There's a mortgage on the home. She used *her* money to build the home. There's a big mortgage on the summer cabin, which she bought with her money. But it is community property. She and her husband and another drunk own the islands. My vague knowledge of the law tells me that any one partner is responsible for all the debts of the partnership. You better investigate it and draw up a reasonable property agreement. If you don't, I'll tell my patient to offer the firm that holds the note for $200,000 to sell her share of the business for one dollar. They'll grab it and put in their own manager. They'll foreclose." I also told the wife she would have to earn the respect of her children after putting up with that husband for so long. She would also have to sell the house, since her husband would buy one in that neighborhood. He did.

* * *

H: We started on the issue of when you choose to see two people at once rather than one. Is there anything that you would *have* to see two people at once for?

E: I usually meet the couple out in the other room. I almost invariably ask them, "Well, which one of you wants to see me first, or do you want to see me together?" Then I watch their facial and head behavior. When I see them looking at each other as if to say, "Won't you please come in with me," then I invite both of them in. If the husband looks at me in shocked horror and points to his wife with a gesture or a mannerism that she's the one that should come in, then I look over at her to see if she is pointing at him as the one who should come in. If so, I invite both of them in. If he points at her and she looks expectant, I take her first. Sometimes it's the husband first. Now and then the husband says, "Before you see my wife I want to see you." Sometimes the wife says, "Before you see my husband I want to have a talk with you." Now, not always do I abide by that, because sometimes I tell them, "All right, but suppose for my better understanding I see both of you together for five, six minutes and then I'll see one of you." The reason for that is if they're too dictatorial about who I am to see first, or they're trying to take charge, I take charge. I say five or six minutes, or sometimes three or four minutes.

H: Then do you stick to that?

E: Yes. I may prolong the interview to 15, 20 minutes, but almost always I abide by the three or four minutes. Because that is the better thing to do. Then I can send them out and again make the choice at the end of three or four minutes. You see, by saying three or four minutes, or "I'll see one of you for two or three minutes," you see, you always limit it. And you give yourself the opportunity of constituting the procedure.

H: Well, do you think there's any sort of a problem where you would have to have both husband and wife in at the same time to solve?

E: Now and then where there are two strongly paranoid reactions, one against the other, you want to start your interview with the two, and then you define immediately your role.

H: How do you do that?

E: It's very simple. Let's say for an hour the husband says a lot of paranoid stuff, maybe very subtle. You turn to the wife and you say, "He actually believes that, and he's sincere in his statements, isn't he?" Having said that, she thinks, "He's on *my* side." The husband thinks, "He's on *her* side." So then I turn around and I say, "Now for courtesy's sake, let's hear a few comments from the wife." She will then retaliate with subtle paranoia, because she's been put on the defensive. And I turn to the husband and I make exactly the same remark. (Laughter) The wife suddenly thinks, "He's on my side, and he's on my husband's side." The husband reacts that way. I give them just time enough, and I say, "Now, you've come to me for help. You certainly want me to view sympathetically both sides of this so that we can reach the *actual* truth. I'm certain that both of you are unafraid of the actual truth." You see, I define the actual truth as my view of it. I've got them both on my side, or both think that I'm on their side. Then all of a sudden they realize that I'm on the side of the actual truth with their whole-hearted cooperation.

H: In general, you feel that working with them you should manage to form a coalition with the both of them, or be on both of their sides.

E: Usually. Now and then you take an entirely different attitude. As the complaint starts from the most vociferous one, and you see how utterly unreasonable that person is going to be, you turn to the other, and you state, "He really sincerely believes all of that; he's convinced of it. You know that a great deal of it, possibly all of it, probably just a great deal of it, is not soundly based. And you want him to know fully everything that is soundly based. You want him to discard everything that isn't, just as he wants to discard everything that really doesn't fit." So you've justified the vociferous one, you've asked for an absolutely objective attitude by the other, but you've also told the vociferous one that you're going to reject all that isn't so, and he's got to agree with you all the way along. Now this sounds as if I am deliberately directing and controlling. All I'm really doing is making it possible for the other person to order his own thinking and his own views. I'm merely pointing out to him, "Here are a few dozen other roads to travel that you didn't notice on the way." I'm making him become aware of the fact that there are other possible understandings. I think the best way of illustrating this is various reasoning puzzles.

CHAPTER 7

Changing Views and Interview Technique

1959. Present were Milton H. Erickson, Jay Haley, and John Weakland.

E: Many people, when they try to solve a problem, stay within the confines of the situation. If you can get them to step outside, you are showing them, "you can step beyond the immediate confines of that emotional problem." All of a sudden they realize there are other views, other possibilities, other understandings. You're merely telling them, or forcing them, to step beyond the immediate confines of that emotional configuration. There's nothing wrong about that. You can prolong therapy until accidentally they step beyond the configuration.

H: Can you give an example of that?

E: Yes. Harold told me all the afternoon, in a repetitious way, about what a nice, sweet wife he had. He just couldn't understand her. He didn't know what their trouble was. He told me that every time he had to go out of town on a trip, his wife got lonesome and some of his friends dropped in. He enjoyed having his friends over, he enjoyed having his wife not lonesome. He mentioned the fact that a friend left his tube of toothpaste on the bathroom sink, left a discarded razor blade there, a different razor than he had. He kept on telling me that story of his adjustments with his wife, their constant quarreling and friction, and of the fact that his wife had pubic lice because of her social service work in a poor section of town.

Finally, after he told me that story about half a dozen times, he said, "You know, if my wife were any other woman, I'd say that she was having affairs." I said, "In what way does your wife differ from other women?" He said, "My God, my wife *is* any other woman!" Then he told me precisely the same story, with a recognition of what that tube of toothpaste in the bathroom meant. What that razor blade discarded there, and detail after detail. I had already known about the affairs; she had been privately my patient. She wanted him to become aware of it so they could either break up or reestablish their marriage on a sound basis. Their marriage worked out very happily. They have children grown now. He's been continuously employed, for heaven's sakes, at least 25 years, in the same place. That realization, that beautiful recitation, item after item.

H: You were giving that as an example of prolonging an interview until he accidentally discovered it.

E: I prolonged it. I made him tell me that story beginning about 1 o'clock in the afternoon. He gave all the details without recognizing their significance. About how Joe, Ray or John would come over and visit his wife on the weekends. The way he told the story implied that Joe had left at dinner time, come back on Sunday morning, left at dinner time. That they had listened to records, and so on. One detail after another. But always inclusive. Of both doing the breakfast dishes. I wonder if she ate two breakfasts? That strange and different kind of toothpaste, with no recognition. That went on until he made that observation, about 6 o'clock, "If my wife were any other woman." "In what way does she differ from other women?" Which is stepping way out of the configuration, and he took a view. And he's a Ph.D. in psychology.

H: How do you see that statement, "In what way does she differ from other women?" as taking him outside of the context?

E: We weren't discussing his problem. This is a general philosophical question, "How does his wife differ from other women?" That's all. He first started on a purely objective, philosophical basis, when he suddenly realized, "My God, she *is* other women!" All that afternoon I had been hoping that he would say something wherein I could ask that kind of a question. That's why I let him repeat his story over and over again. Always hopefully listening for some little remark where I could yank him outside of that constricted situation. Always in therapy whenever you get a chance to pull a patient away from a situation so they can take an objective view, then there's nothing they can do about those new understandings they developed.

W: What do you mean there's nothing they can do about them?

E: Well, once he recognized that his wife was "other women," he went through that entire story, every detail, and identified it correctly. I made an appointment for him and his wife the next day. I told his wife, "Now you keep very quiet. Your husband has got something to say." He went through the entire story, detail by detail, coldly, deliberately, identifying the toothpaste tube, the razor blades, the breakfast dishes, the different kind of breakfast foods that he had never eaten. He enumerated some grocery bills where she had charged for something for a breakfast so that she could cook a special breakfast for one of her boyfriends. Another time another of her boyfriends. He had recognized all of that unconsciously, had repressed it completely, but he had kept it in catalog fashion.

H: You wanted his confrontation of her to occur in your presence then?

E: Oh yes. He went right straight through the whole array of instances.

W: You had heard a good bit by that time; this was about the third telling.

E: I had also heard from her. (Laughter)

H: Well now, did you instruct him not to talk about this with his wife when he went home? But to come in the next day and talk about it with her here?

E: Yes. I had told her that I was seeing her husband on that particular Saturday afternoon, and that I thought she had better be out of town that Saturday afternoon. Stay out of town until Sunday morning. Sunday morning come in and telephone. So I gave her an appointment for Sunday morning and him an appointment for Sunday morning, for confrontation. He went through the entire thing while she sat there mute, obviously horribly distressed, amazed at the acuity of his unconscious knowledge.

When he finished, I told her, "You can go out in the other room, and I'll ask your husband what should be done next." See, the confrontation, she had wanted that. Then after he had confronted her and gone through it, and got that tacit acknowledgment, her silence, sending her out. Then Joe said, "What should I do?" "You have a lot of thinking to do. Do you want to continue your marriage, do you want a divorce, do you want a separation?" He said, "I love her very much. I'd like to put all of this in the past." I said, "That's an impulsive utterance. Suppose you come back here a week from now. In the meantime, don't see her. Do all of your own thinking all by yourself."

So he went home. His wife went to a hotel. I told

her about the appointment in a week's time. The next week when I saw them I beat Joe to the punch, because he didn't know he was going to need to do it. When the wife came in, the same hour he did, and sat down, I said, "Before we begin the interview that's to determine your future, there's one question I want to ask: When you were living at the hotel this past week, has your bed been occupied only by you?" He said, "I knew there was some question I would have to ask her, but try as hard as I could I couldn't figure it out." She said, "I was tempted several times, but I figured that, well, Joe might want me back. I knew I wanted to come back. I didn't want to gamble for a few minutes' pleasure."

H: Presumably that put them back together?

E: Yes. Very little discussion about the affairs. I had to ask essentially all of the personal questions. Some I asked of him, some I asked of her. I said, "Joe, your good friend Jack . . . " He said, "He *used* to be a good friend. He will get the go-by next time I see him. I'll tell him very simply, 'Keep out of my sight.' If he asks me why, I'll tell him that 'I think you are a cowardly son of a bitch,' or something like that." I asked the wife, "What about Bill?" See, there were half a dozen college men she was having affairs with. I had a good description of all of them from her. I had known which ones Joe would emphasize. So I asked Joe about those he emphasized, then I asked her about the others – just so they were disposed of.

H: That was the only discussion of the past affairs?

E: A year later when I saw them I asked them separately if the matter had come up again. Joe said, "No, it's crossed my mind several times, but Ann and I have been planning our family. Going into the matter of our living expenses, our economics, the amount of money we would save, what special pleasures we can have that will permit us to save money." I really ought to write and find out if they added any children besides those two daughters.

H: Well now, you wouldn't assume that it was necessary at all for them to express their feelings about this?

E: He said, "My God, she isn't any different from any other woman!" and he retold that story. All afternoon he had been sitting there placidly narrating. With that sudden eruption of insight he was yelling, waving his hands, jumping up and down. It was a very violent catharsis. When I had him confront his wife – that set jaw, that utterly intense voice, as he enumerated item by item. She sat there obediently – "Just sit down and be quiet," and I meant be quiet. Because Joe made some little errors in his stories, and she had to take those errors. (Laughter)

H: You didn't want her defending herself.

E: No, you see, if you allow her to defend herself, then she's going to transform the situation. Now Joe's errors she had to accept and be culpable of those items too. Now how would it work when she had to passively admit her culpability for *those* things if she wanted to fight? When she won't defend herself, let her emotion be, "I might as well take that discredit." In other words, it was self-punishment, cudgeling herself with the weapon, the cudgel, her husband had offered. So it was an emotional catharsis for her.

For a number of years I met them regularly at professional meetings. A goodly number of years later I was talking to Joe, and we reminisced about various things, which included things relating to just preceding and just following. Joe recognized, "Yes, that was the time that I discovered my wife was just another woman." She, of course, has told me they had been very happy in their marriage. Those two little girls obviously came from a happy home.

H: Well now, what you did was see them separately, and then bring them together for the confrontation, and immediately separate them again. After he confronted her with all this, you didn't want arguing between the two of them.

E: I didn't want an argument because then they go back to previous patterns of thinking. If there's an argument, he will think, "Well now, if I had said this." She will think, "If I could have answered this." Then it's a reaffirmation of past patterns. If you bring about the confrontation and then the separation, there's no possibility then of an argument, except after everything's cooled down. That's a totally different thing than the red-hot situation.

W: You said you gave each of them an appointment for that same time. Did *they* know that the other was going to be here until they got here?

E: No.

W: So they also couldn't get primed for that.

E: It was none of their business what *I* was doing. They each had a major task to perform all by themselves. They each came in expecting just to see me. Absolutely unprepared. Then, of course, in that situation with me, it wasn't too difficult to do – to keep them from going back to past, because I wanted to know about the future, not the past.

W: So you set up the situation that you wanted and prevented them both from getting set for it beforehand or rehashing it afterward.

E: Yes. Because I see no sense in a rehash. They had all the facts, so did I. The only question was, "Is this the termination of your relationship, or is it the beginning of a new one?" If it's termination, period. If it's the beginning of the new, what do you want in this new relationship? In other words, are you moving out of that old house into a new one? If you're moving out, all right, let's not talk about scrubbing the kitchen, the basement, and so on. What do you want in the new house? Now that's a figure of speech, or an analogy, I use quite often. "So you're going to move out of the old house, and leave all of the old furniture there. What kind of view do you want from the new one? It ought to be in a different part of town, with a different view, a different house entirely, with different furniture, different arrangements. Now what do you want in the new house?"

H: You wouldn't assume in that situation that she would need to, oh, defend herself by pointing out how her husband had not provided what she needed, or something like that, so that she had to have affairs.

E: One of the questions I put to her was, "What kind of lovemaking do you want in the future from Joe? The frequency, the duration?" These were the simple questions she had to answer.

H: Well, did you presume that when she laid out what she wanted, he would then deliver that?

E: No. I pointed out to her, "Now you've stated what you want. What does Joe want?" You know I always use analogies. I don't know which particular one, but one that comes to my mind is, "Suppose Joe invites you to have dinner in a restaurant. You know what you want when you pick up the menu. Joe knows what he wants. There's *one* thing that's going to decide it—the money in the wallet. A reality situation. So you both accommodate your wishes to the reality possibilities. Joe has so much capacity to love in the way that you want; you have so much capacity to love in the way that he wants. An intelligent attitude in a restaurant in which you can get a meal." (Laughter)

* * *

H: When you have two people in the room, and you want to engineer the conversation either to encourage one of them to do more talking, or to encourage one of them to shut up so the other one can, what procedure do you use to do that?

E: You mean when you can't tell them directly?

H: Yes. When you tell the wife you want to get the husband's point of view, and the wife goes on rattling. Then you ask her to be quiet because you'd like to have the husband's point of view, and she goes right on. What do you do then?

E: I tell them, "You know, I still want your husband's point of view, and you keep right on talking. I know it's because of your eagerness to enable me to understand. But do you happen to have a lipstick? Will you take it out of your purse? Now this will sound ridiculous to you, but suppose you hold that lipstick like this. Just keep it right there (against the lips) and I'm going to ask your husband some questions; notice how your lips want to move. I think you'll find it very interesting." I know one woman got so fascinated watching the quivering of her lips on that lipstick. (Laughter)

H: She wouldn't dare move them.

E: But you've given her a legitimate use for her lips. They don't quite understand. It's amusing.

H: You mentioned that one of the ways you get – usually the man – to say what's on his mind when he's not saying anything is to mention his courage. Do you have other ways to bring them into it? If you've got a couple and one of them isn't talking and obviously should be included.

E: "I don't know how many things you noted that should be restated." Then you turn to the other one, let the other one talk, and again there are some more things that really need restating. Third time around, "Have you decided exactly what way to restate some of that first thing?" You frustrate them by turning to the talker. You know that frustration of people in this matter of speech. I can think of one of my patients with an aphasia: "What is your name? How old are you? Where do you live? What town did you come from? Which baseball team do you want to support?" Each time the patient would try to answer the question, but before the mouth movements could get under way, the next question was asked. Next question. A very, very effective way of breaking it down. The patient is going to be mute, you ask a question, just start to pause, don't give them a chance to answer, ask the next question. Give them a chance, but don't wait long enough to permit them to answer. Hit them with the next question. You're so earnest, and it frustrates them until finally they say, "Will you shut up. The answer is . . . "

H: It's the same with suggesting to one to restate it and then shifting away before they have a chance to make a comment.

E: Yes. In teaching medical students, I use that sort of technique on the hesitant ones.

H: You mean you ask them a question and then don't give them a chance to answer?

E: That's right.

H: Well, there's another point of view on that; somebody hesitating to answer you is a way of handling you, which they can't very well do if you're going right to the next question. You force them to handle you differently when you do that.

E: They've got to handle you differently. The only opportunity that's being given them is on your terms. They've got to let loose of *their* way. They've got to grab hold of something new, and the only thing new is what you're presenting. "Now this is your first interview with me. You tell me that you want to relate some very painful things. In other words, I judge you mean some things that you'd rather not tell me. I think you ought not to tell me those things you just can't endure telling me. Tell me the things that you *can*, with the least possible amount of pain, and be sure you hold back the things you can't bear to tell me." They start in relating and at the end of the hour say, "But I've told you all the things I can't bear to tell you." What do they do? It was always a question, "Can I bear to tell this or not? I'm free to withhold it. But, oh, I guess I could tell this one." They always vote in favor of telling.

One woman told me, "I've been to several other psychiatrists. It takes me at least 10 to 20 hours before I can unburden myself. I usually spend 10 to 20 hours wasting my time talking about things that are nonsensical." So I told her, "All right, let's make sure of this. I want you to withhold the thing you can't endure telling me." At the end of the hour, she said, "You know, I've told you more than I've told anybody else ever." Each time you see them vote, "Oh, I'll withhold the rest, not this, I don't need to withhold this, I'll withhold that." So it is a constant narration, always postponing the withholding.

H: I imagine you could handle a couple that way. By saying to them, "I want you not to say here what would be painful to the other person."

E: Oh yes. "Now I want to hear both of your stories, but there certainly are things that you are going to withhold. You're going to withhold it because you'd rather let your wife tell me than tell me yourself."

H: That's a slippery one.

E: I know. Is it unfair to ask them to make up their mind? Will you, or will you not – or do you want someone else to tell it? It's a facing of reality.

H: Yes. Well, it's assuming it will be told and putting the question on who's going to tell it, not on whether it will be told or not.

E: Yes. Well, what did they come here for anyway? One of my patients has been married 14 times; she came in and told me, "I need your help. There are some things I'm going to hold out on you. It's got nothing to do with the situation. I'm going to hold it out, and I don't want you to pry." I said, "All right, I won't, but if you tell me spontaneously, don't accuse me of prying." (Laughter) During that same hour she said, "I had no intention of telling you about my two first marriages. But somehow or other when you told me that I didn't have to tell you anything that I didn't really want to, and then you told me that I couldn't hold you responsible for any of my spontaneous telling, it had the effect of making me feel I could tell you anything." Her husband doesn't know that she's been married 14 times previously.

H: You do get them. (Laughs)

E: He thinks she's been married twice before.

W: Well, she certainly has.

E: Yes. She made me promise not to tell her husband. She wasn't going to tell me, but somehow it leaked out during the interview. Then I pointed out to her that her husband was being awfully patient and kind with her, that he had allowed her to forge checks and he'd made good on it. She lost her temper and wrecked his car, and he was a hardworking man, and she chased out with other men repeatedly. Her husband was having a hard time trying to make up his mind whether or not he wanted to stay with her. Didn't she think she ought to tell him about the other 12 marriages?

She said "No." I said, "Well, that's your answer, stick to it."

H: You wouldn't encourage her to do it?

E: Do you think she took orders from men? (Laughs)

H: So did she tell him?

E: She told him.

H: This was partly because you told her to stick to her answer?

E: Yes. She showed me. I had interviewed her husband before. When she told him, he said, "So you've been married a total of 14 times. With how many of them did you commit forgery?" She told him. "With how many of them did you run out with other men?" She told him. He said, "All right. I married you, and I'm in love with you even if you are a louse. Any more forgery, any more running out, and I'm going to get a divorce on the basis you withheld vital information from me." She straightened out, she's afraid of losing that fifteenth husband. I liked the guy. He was a nice, strong character. He felt his strength, and he didn't want to exercise it on his nice, sweet, mistaken, neurotic wife who couldn't be blamed because she had had two unhappy marriages.

W: But with 14 the picture looked a little different.

E: The picture looked different. He took a totally different attitude. All I did was stick to her assertion. It was her weakness that broke her down, not my advice.

W: Let's talk more about a couple giving each other a hard time.

E: And each striving not to give the other a hard time?

W: Well, sure. I assume at some level they're always trying that too.

E: Yes, at some level. I've told people to come in the office and *really* give each other a hard time. Really, honest-to-goodness, give the other a hard time. The other sits there and takes it. It's one of the nicest ways of getting a husband over on his wife's side of the fence, and getting the wife over on her husband's side of the fence.

H: Well, you touched upon getting two people involved in a self-punishment deal. Can you give any other examples of where you get two of them involved in something like that?

E: Yes. A woman was an alcoholic, a pretty bad alcoholic. A concealed drinker. She hid all of her drinks. Her husband worked in the office every day. And that nightly battle because she was drunk and he was infuriated. His idea of a *good* weekend was leaning back in an easy chair and reading *Business Week*, or some such journal as that, *The Wall Street Journal*, the Sunday *New York Times* from cover to cover. That was his idea of weekend enjoyment. Her idea of a weekend enjoyment was to go out in the yard, work with the flowers, and when nobody was looking, slip that bottle of whiskey hidden in the ground up to her mouth. She really enjoyed gardening. She also enjoyed the whiskey.

So I got the two of them here in the office, and I pointed out that he came home every evening and laboriously tried to figure out where she had hidden her bottle of whiskey. She took a gleeful delight in hiding it. My statement was, if he couldn't find it, she was entitled to empty it the next day. I let them play that game for a little while. It isn't a good game. But he didn't like that hunting; she got too much joy out of it, penalizing him. But you know it robbed her of the privilege of hiding secretly. This was purposeful hiding. Not that guilty, shameful, sneaking hiding. So it took some of the joy out of hiding her liquor.

H: Was he hunting for it when he came home, before your directive?

E: Oh, he used to rage around the house trying to figure

It was an unlovely situation for everybody, but it salvaged the marriage. Husband and wife got together and decided to ship that nasty maid to another state, where she had some relatives. I also arranged that the wife force the maid to pack the husband's clothes and carry them out to the front yard so he could go off and live by himself. She threw him out of the house with the maid carrying the suitcases out. Then she had the maid bring them back in, unpack them, and then repack them and carry them out again.

In this way I arranged that the wife express pleasure in her power and also arranged that the husband could come back at her bidding. With this arrangement, he could return when she let him, and she decided to let him come back. She told me to notify her husband that he could return. Instead of doing so, I said, "Yes, I can tell him to come back, any third party can tell him to do that, the mailman can tell him." She was tremendously relieved. She wrote the letter to her husband, and the third party, the mailman, delivered it. I didn't wish to be the third party, but I knew there should be one. A third party that was an extension of her.

H: You assume that if they got back together without this there would be a sore spot that could be brought up again and again.

E: It was brought up a couple of years later. The maid came back and applied for her job. (Laughter) There were two allies who came barging into this office. "What are we going to do with that stupid idiot?" "We." There was a *we-ness*.

INDEX